Thai for Beginners

by
Benjawan Poomsan Becker
(เบญจวรรณ ภูมิแสน เบคเกอร์)

PAIBOON

PP

PUBLISHING

ภาษาไทย

- 299 BAHT -

Thai for Beginners
Copyright ©1995 by Paiboon Publishing
(สำนักพิมพ์ไพบูลย์ภูมิแสน)
Printed in Thailand

Paiboon Poomsan Publishing
582 Amarinniwate Village 2
Sukhapiban Road 1, Bungkum
Bangkok 10230
THAILAND
☎   662-509-8632
Fax 662-519-5437

สำนักพิมพ์ไพบูลย์ภูมิแสน
582 หมู่บ้านอัมรินทร์นิเวศน์ 2
ถ. สุขาภิบาล 1 เขตบึงกุ่ม
ก.ท.ม. 10230
☎   662-509-8632
โทรสาร 662-519-5437

E-Mail: paiboon@thailao.com
www.thailao.com

Paiboon Publishing
PMB 192, 1442A Walnut Street
Berkeley, California USA 94709
☎   1-510-848-7086
Fax 1-510-848-4521
E-Mail: paiboon@thailao.com
www.thailao.com

Cover and graphic design by Randy Kincaid
Cover picture: Kanjana Saen-ong Kincaid
Edited by Craig Becker, Ron Colvin II, Hal Schuster

ISBN 1-887521-00-3

Printed by Chulalongkorn University Printing House
February, 2002 (4504-188/3,000(2))
http://www.cuprint.chula.ac.th

Introduction

Many people interested in learning the Thai language have trouble finding a good textbook. **Thai for Beginners** solves that problem.

Thai for Beginners teaches the basic four language skills—speaking, listening (with the cassette tapes), reading and writing. The first part of each lesson teaches vocabulary and sentence structure. A vocabulary list with Thai spelling, transliteration and definitions in English appears at the beginning of each chapter.

The transliteration system assists you with pronunciation while you are learning the Thai alphabet. Each student must learn to properly pronounce the tones either by listening to the tapes or with the help of a good Thai teacher. Someone should listen to and correct your pronunciation, especially during your early days of learning the language.

Often, beginning students of Thai only want to learn conversation. Perhaps, learning the alphabet seems too difficult when their main goal is to talk to someone using the Thai language. This is a big mistake!

The phonetic Thai alphabet will assist even basic conversation. Using the Thai writing system develops speaking and listening skills as well as reading and writing. Wean yourself off of transliteration as soon as possible. You won't regret the extra effort spent learning the Thai writing system.

The second part of each lesson teaches basic reading and writing of the Thai language. It provides a guided step by step introduction to the consonants, vowels, tone rules, and other features of the language.

Written Thai uses no space between words. In this text, however, we often separate the words with a space to help you read the Thai script more quickly.

The appendix features an introduction to the Thai alphabet and a summary of the Thai writing system for quick reference.

Characteristics of the Thai language different from English include:

* There are no variant or plural forms for adjectives and nouns.

* Adjectives follow the noun.
  In Thai we say 'car red' (*rót sǐi dɛɛng*)
  instead of 'red car'.

* There are no verb conjugations in Thai. We understand tenses from the context or from adverbs of time.

* There are no articles (a, an, the).

* There is no verb 'to be' with adjectives.
  'She is beautiful' would be 'She beautiful.' (*kǎo sǔai*)

* Thai usually omits the subject of a sentence when it is understood from the context.

* Thai is a tonal language.
  If the tone is not correct, you won' t be easily understood, even if your pronunciation is otherwise perfect.

This book is designed for beginners and those who want to improve their basic Thai. Help in learning more advanced conversation and reading can be found in *"Thai for Intermediate Learners."*

The Thai language grows increasingly more important. Not only is Thailand a favorite vacation paradise, it enjoys one of the world's fastest growing economies. These factors, combined with the Thai people's legendary friendliness, make Thai a language well worth learning!

Table of Contents

Guide to Pronunciation   7

Lesson 1   17
Greetings; polite particles; yes-no questions;
personal pronouns; cardinal and ordinal numbers;
the Thai writing system; consonant classes;
determining tones in written Thai;
middle consonants; long vowels; tone marks

Lesson 2   39
'bpen', 'yùu' (to be); more vowels; live and dead
syllables; tone rules for middle consonants

Lesson 3   61
Colors; 'jà' (future tense); 'dâai' (can); more vowels;
complex vowels; final consonants;
Seven vowels that change their forms;
tone rules for middle consonants (cont.)

Lesson 4   87
Telling time; high consonants;
tone rules for high consonants

Lesson 5   107
Days of the week; months; tone marks with
high consonants; low consonants introduced

Lesson 6   127
'ao', 'yàak' (to want); 'gamlang' (to be ... ing);
tone rules for low consonants

Lesson 7 147
'dâi-yin' (to hear); 'jam' (to remember);
'nɔɔn-làp'(to fall asleep); 'mɔɔng' (to look);
tone rules for low consonants (cont.)

Lesson 8 167
Body parts; everyday life; special ฮ; silent ห

Lesson 9 183
Family and kinship terms; occupations; animals;
how to use ใ; other features of written Thai

Lesson 10 207
Comparisons; adjectives; classifiers

Appendix I 237
Summary of the Thai Writing System

Appendix II 253
Test and Writing Exercise Answers

Guide to Pronunciation

Tones

Because Thai is a tonal language, its pronunciation presents new challenges for English speakers. If the tone is wrong, you will not be easily understood even if everything else is correct. Thai uses five tones. For example, to pronounce a rising tone, your voice starts at a low pitch and goes up (much like asking a question in English). The phonetic transliteration in this text book uses tone marks over the vowels to show the tone for each word. Note that the tone marks used for transliteration are different from those used in Thai script.

Tone Marks (Transliteration)

Tone	Tone symbol	Example
mid	*None*	maa
low	`	màa
falling	^	mâa
high	´	máa
rising	ˇ	mǎa

Vowels

Most Thai vowels have two versions, short and long. Short vowels are clipped and cut off at the end. Long ones are drawn out. This book shows short vowels with a single letter and long vowels with double letters ('a' for short; 'aa' for long).

The 'ʉ' has no comparable sound in English. Try saying 'u' while spreading your lips in as wide a smile as possible. If the sound you are making is similar to one you might have uttered after stepping on something disgusting, you are probably close!

Short & Long Vowels

a	*like* a *in* Alaska	fan - *teeth*
aa	*like* a *in* father	maa - *come*
i	*like* i *in* tip	sìp - *ten*
ii	*like* ee *in* see	sìi - *four*
u	*like* oo *in* boot	kun - *you*
uu	*like* u *in* ruler	sŭun - *zero*
ʉ	*like* u *in* ruler, but with a smile	nὓng - *one*
ʉʉ	*like* ʉ *but longer*	mʉʉ - *hand*
e	*like* e *in* pet	sèt - *finish*
ee	*like* a *in* pale	pleeng-*song*
ɛ	*like* a *in* cat	lέ - *and*
ɛɛ	*like* a *in* sad	dɛɛng - *red*
ə	*like* er *in* teacher without the r *sound*	lə́ - *dirty*
əə	*like* ə *but longer*	jəə - *meet*
o	*like* o *in* note	jon - *poor*
oo	*like* o *in* go	joon -*robber*
ɔ	*like* au *in* caught	gɔ̀ - *island*
ɔɔ	*like* aw *in* law	nɔɔn - *sleep*

Complex Vowels

The following dipthongs are combinations of the above vowels.

ai	mâi - *not*		aai	saai - *sand*
ao	mao - *drunk*		aao	kâao - *rice*
ia	bia - *beer*		iao	nĭao - *sticky*
ua	dtua- *body*		uai	ruai - *rich*
ʉa	rʉa - *boat*		ʉai	nὓai - *tired*
ɔi	nɔ̀i - *little*		ɔɔi	kɔɔi - *wait*
ooi	dooi - *by*		əəi	nəəi - *butter*
ui	kui - *chat*		iu	hĭu - *hungry*
eo	reo - *fast*		eeo	eeo - *waist*
ɛo	tĕo - *row*		ɛɛo	lέɛo - *already*

Consonants

b	*as in* <u>b</u>aby	bin -	*fly*
ch	*as in* <u>ch</u>in	chûu -	*name*
d	*as in* <u>d</u>oll	duu -	*look*
f	*as in* <u>f</u>un	fai -	*fire*
g	*as in* <u>g</u>old	gin -	*eat*
h	*as in* <u>h</u>oney	hâa -	*five*
j	*as in* <u>j</u>et	jèt -	*seven*
k	*as in* <u>k</u>iss	kon -	*person*
l	*as in* <u>l</u>ove	ling -	*monkey*
m	*as in* <u>m</u>oney	mii -	*have*
n	*as in* <u>n</u>eed	naa -	*rice field*
p	*as in* <u>p</u>retty	pan -	*thousand*
r	*rolled like the Scottish* <u>r</u>	rian -	*study*
s	*as in* <u>s</u>ex	sìi -	*four*
t	*as in* <u>t</u>ender	tam -	*do*
w	*as in* <u>w</u>oman	wan -	*day*
y	*as in* <u>y</u>ou	yaa -	*medicine*
ng	*as in* ri<u>ng</u>ing	ngaan -	*work*
dt	*as in* s<u>t</u>op	dtaa -	*eye*
bp	*as in* s<u>p</u>ot	bpai -	*go*

The /dt/ sound lies between the /d/ and the /t/. Similarly, the /bp/ is between /b/ and /p/. (In linguistic terms, they are both unvoiced and unaspirated.) Unlike English, /ng/ frequently occurs at the beginning of words in Thai. Thai people often do not pronounce the /r/, replacing it with /l/ ('rian' will sound like 'lian'). When the /r/ is part of a consonant cluster, it is often dropped completely. ('kráp' will sound like 'káp'.)

Practice saying the words below while your teacher listens. Then have your teacher say the words and see if you can hear the tones correctly.

Mid	Low	Falling	High	Rising
maa	-	-	máa	mǎa
to come			horse	dog
mai	mài	mâi	mái	mǎi
mile	new	no, not	..... , right?	silk
glai	-	glâi	-	-
far		near		
sai	sài	sâi	-	sǎi
a kind of fish trap	to wear	intestine		clear
paa	pàa	pâa	-	pǎa
to take along	to cut, to split	cloth		cliff
kaao	kàao	kâao	-	kǎao
fishy	news	rice		white
-	wàt	-	wát	-
	a cold		temple	
-	sʉ̀a	sʉ̂a	-	sʉ̌a
	mat	shirt		tiger
yaa	yàa	yâa	-	
medicine	"don't"	grandmother, grass		

Practice the Following Words

A. Words with mid tones:

1. dii (ดี) - *good*
2. kon (คน) - *person*
3. jai (ใจ) - *heart*
4. aai (อาย) - *to be shy*
5. kruu (ครู) - *teacher*

B. Words with low tones:

1. nùng (หนึ่ง) - *one*
2. sìi (สี่) - *four*
3. jèt (เจ็ด) - *seven*
4. jà (จะ) - *will*
5. sèt (เสร็จ) - *to finish*

C. Words with falling tones:

1. hâa (ห้า) - *five*
2. gâao (เก้า) - *nine*
3. nîi (นี้) - *this*
4. châi (ใช่) - *correct*
5. mâi (ไม่) - *not, no*

D. Words with high tones:

1. fáa (ฟ้า) - *blue*
2. náam (น้ำ) - *water*
3. chái (ใช้) - *to use*
4. rúu (รู้) - *to know*
5. rák (รัก) - *to love*

E. Words with rising tones:

1. mǎa (หมา) - *dog*
2. sǔung (สูง) - *tall*
3. nǎngsǔu (หนังสือ) - *book*
4. mǔu (หมู) - *pig*
5. kǎao (ขาว) - *white*

More About Tones, Short-Long Vowels, Similar Consonants and Vowel Sounds

When you are not understood, often you are saying the tone wrong. However, the length of the vowel is also very important. Try to get the vowel length correct. This will help you to be understood better while you are still learning to master the tones.
Practice saying the following words.

Different Tone, Different Meaning

1. maa   (มา)   - *to come*

    máa   (ม้า)   - *horse*

    măa   (หมา)   - *dog*

2. mai   (ไมล์)   - *mile*

    mài   (ใหม่)   - *new*

    mâi   (ไม่, ไหม้) - *no, to burn*

    mái   (มั้ย)   - *....., right?*

    măi   (ไหม)   - *silk*

3. kào   (เข่า)   - *knee*

    kâo   (เข้า)   - *to enter*

    káo   (เค้า)   - *he/she*

    kăo   (เขา)   - *animal horn*

4. kaao (คาว)   - *fishy*

    kàao (ข่าว)   - *news*

    kâao (ข้าว)   - *rice*

    kăao (ขาว)   - *white*

5. sii   (ซี)   - *"a particle"*

    sìi   (สี่)   - *four*

    sîi   (ซี่)   - *the classifier for "tooth"*

    sĭi   (สี)   - *color*

6.   glai   (ไกล)   - *far*
       glâi   (ใกล้)   - *near*

7.   sùa   (เสื่อ)   - *mat*
       sûa   (เสื้อ)   - *shirt*
       sǔa   (เสือ)   - *tiger*

8.   baa   (บาร์)   - *bar*
       bàa   (บ่า)   - *shoulder*
       bâa   (บ้า)   - *mad, crazy*

9.   paa   (พา)   - *to take along*
       pàa   (ผ่า)   - *to cut, to split*
       pâa   (ผ้า)   - *cloth*
       pǎa   (ผา)   - *cliff*

10.   bpaa   (ปา)   - *to throw*
       bpàa   (ป่า)   - *forest*
       bpâa   (ป้า)   - *aunt*
       bpǎa   (ป๋า)   - *father (of a Chinese Thai)*

11.   yàak   (อยาก)   - *to want to*
       yâak   (ยาก)   - *difficult*

12.   yaa   (ยา)   - *medicine*
       yàa   (อย่า)   - *don't*
       yâa   (ย่า)   - *grandmother*

13.   bpuu   (ปู)   - *crab*
       bpùu   (ปู่)   - *grandfather*

14.   naa   (นา)   - *rice field*
       nâa   (หน้า)   - *face, season*
       nǎa   (หนา)   - *thick*

15.   mii   (มี)   - *to have*
       mìi   (หมี่)   - *dry noodle*
       mǐi   (หมี)   - *bear*

16. pèt   (เผ็ด)   - *spicy*
     pét   (เพชร)   - *diamond*
17. nai   (ใน)   - *in*
     nǎi   (ไหน)   - *where*
18. wàt   (หวัด)   - *a cold*
     wát   (วัด)   - *temple*
19. sai   (ไซ)   - *a kind of fish trap*
     sài   (ใส่)   - *to put on*
     sâi   (ไส้)   - *intestine*
     sǎi   (ใส)   - *clear*
20. saai (ทราย) - *sand*
     sàai (ส่าย)   - *to shake*
     sáai (ซ้าย)   - *left*
     sǎai (สาย)   - *late*

Short and Long Vowels

1. kǎo   (เขา)   - *horn*   kǎao (ขาว)   - *white*
2. kâo   (เข้า)   - *to enter*   kâao (ข้าว)   - *rice*
3. jan   (จันทร์) - *moon*   jaan (จาน)   - *plate*
4. yang (ยัง)   - *yet*   yaang (ยาง)   - *rubber*
5. kun   (คุณ)   - *you*   kuun (คูณ)   - *to multiply*
6. sǎi   (ใส)   - *clear*   sǎai (สาย)   - *late*
7. mâi   (ไม่)   - *no*   mâai (ม่าย) - *widower*
8. jàk   (จักร)   - *sewing   jàak (จาก)   - *from*
                     machine*
9. nai   (ใน)   - *in*   naai (นาย)   - *Mr.*
10. rao   (เรา)   - *we*   raao (ราว)   - *about*

Similar Sounds

1.   dii *(ดี)*   - *good*   dtii *(ตี)*   - *to hit*
2.   bai *(ใบ)*   - *leaf*   bpai *(ไป)*   - *to go*
3.   nǔu *(หนู)*   - *mouse*   nguu *(งู)*   - *snake*
4.   pèt *(เผ็ด)*   - *spicy*   bpèt *(เป็ด)*   - *duck*
5.   tǔng *(ถุง)*   - *bag*   tǔng *(ถึง)*   - *to*
6.   krûang *(เครื่อง)* - *machine*   krûng *(ครึ่ง)*   - *half*
7.   dao *(เดา)*   - *to guess*   dtao *(เตา)*   - *stove*
8.   nən *(เนิน)*   - *mound, hill*   ngən *(เงิน)*   - *money*
9.   ùut *(อูฐ)*   - *camel*   ùut *(ยืด)*   - *swollen*
10.   glua *(กลัว)*   - *to be afraid*   glua *(เกลือ)*   - *salt*

Practice the Following Sentences

1.   rao tam naa nâa fǒn. *(เราทำนาหน้าฝน)*
        - *We plant rice in the rainy season.*
2.   krai kǎai kài gài. *(ใครขายไข่ไก่)*
        - *Who sells chicken eggs?*
3.   máai mài mâi mâi mái. *(ไม้ใหม่ไม่ไหม้มั้ย)*
        - *New wood doesn't burn, does it?*
4.   bâan yùu glâi glâi. mâi glai. *(บ้านอยู่ใกล้ๆ ไม่ไกล)*
        - *The house is pretty near, not far.*
5.   sûa yùu bon sùa. *(เสื้ออยู่บนเสื่อ)*
        - *The shirt is on the mat.*
        sǔa yùu bon sùa. *(เสืออยู่บนเสื่อ)*
        - *The tiger is on the mat.*
        sûa yùu bon sǔa. *(เสื้ออยู่บนเสือ)*
        - *The shirt is on the tiger.*

Irregular Tones

The tone pronunciation of some common words has evolved and they are now usually pronounced differently from the way they are written in Thai script.

For example:

ดิฉัน (dì-chǎn) *is usually pronounced* ดิชั้น (dì-chán).

เขา (kǎo) *is usually pronounced* เค้า (káo).

ไหม (mǎi) *(the question particle) is usually pronounced*
มั้ย (mái).

In our transliteration system, we give the pronunciation most commonly used by modern Thai speakers.

For example:

ดิฉัน *is transcribed as* dì-chán.

เขา *is transcribed as* káo.

ไหม *is transcribed as* mái.

For poly-syllabic words, in normal speech, the tone of the initial syllable tends to become a mid tone.

For example:

à-rai *sounds like* a-rai *in normal speech.*

sà-wàtdii *sounds like* sa-wàtdii *in normal speech.*

Lesson 1

Greetings; polite particles; yes-no questions;
personal pronouns; cardinal and ordinal numbers;
the Thai writing system; consonant classes;
determining tones in written Thai;
middle consonants; long vowels; tone marks

bòtîi nùng   บทที่ ๑   *Lesson 1*

kamsàp   คำศัพท์   *Vocabulary*

pŏm	ผม	I, me *(male speaker)*
dì-chán/chán	ดิฉัน(ดิชั้น) / ฉัน	I, me *(female speaker)*
kun	คุณ	you
chûu	ชื่อ	name
sà-wàtdii	สวัสดี	"Good day."[1]
sà-baai dii mái/sà-baai dii rǔu		"How are you?"
สบายดีไหม/สบายดีหรือ		
sà-baai dii	สบายดี	to be fine
yindii tîi dâai rúu-jàk		Nice to meet you.
ยินดีที่ได้รู้จัก		
chên-gan	เช่นกัน	Same here.
kɔ̌ɔ-tôot	ขอโทษ	Excuse me.
mâi bpenrai	ไม่เป็นไร	It doesn't matter.[2]
kɔ̀ɔpkun	ขอบคุณ	Thank you.
lâ	ล่ะ	"What about .....?"
kráp	ครับ	polite particle *(male speaker)*[3]
kâ/ ká	ค่ะ/ คะ	polite particle *(female speaker)*[3]
nǎngsǔu	หนังสือ	book
nǎngsǔu-pim	หนังสือพิมพ์	newspaper
naa-lí-gaa	นาฬิกา	watch, clock
bpàak-gaa	ปากกา	pen
dinsɔ̌ɔ	ดินสอ	*din saw*	pencil
grà-bpǎo	กระเป๋า	*grah bow*	bag
pěentîi	แผนที่	*pan tee*	map
sà-mùt	สมุด	*sah mood*	notebook
nîi	นี่	*Knee*	this
nân	นั่น		that

nôon โน่น	that (further away)
à-rai อะไร	what
châi ใช่	yes
mâi ไม่	no, not
mái ไหม	a question particle[4]
châi mái ใช่ไหม	..... right?
rǔu/rú หรือ/รึ	or
gɔ̂ɔ ก็	also
kâo-jai mái เข้าใจไหม	Understand?
kâo-jai เข้าใจ	(I) understand.
mâi kâo-jai ไม่เข้าใจ	(I) don't understand.

1. sà-wàtdii *can be used in greeting or leave-taking at any time of day or night.*

2. mâi bpenrai *has the following meanings: it doesn't matter; that's all right; not at all; it's nothing; never mind; don't mention it; forget it; you're welcome, etc.*

3. "kráp *and* kâ/ ká" *are used as:*
   a. *polite particles at the end of statements and questions.*
   b. *"yes" — when answering a question.*
   c. *"yes?" — as a reply when called or spoken to.*
   d. *particles placed after a name, title or kin term to address or attract the attention of someone.*

4. mái (ไหม) *and* châi mái (ใช่ไหม) *are question particles placed at the end of sentences to form yes-no questions.*

   e.g. dii   = *good*

   dii mái = *Is it good?*

Conversation 1

Supa: sà-wàtdii kâ.

สุภา: สวัสดี   ค่ะ

      Hello.

John: sà-wàtdii kráp.

จอห์น: สวัสดี   ครับ

      Hello.

Supa: chán chนน sù-paa. kun chนน à-rai ká.

สุภา: ฉัน ชื่อ   สุภา   คุณ ชื่อ อะไร คะ

      My name is Supa.   What's your name?   — *Know*

John: pǒm chนน jɔɔn kráp.   yin-dii tîi dâai rúu-jàk.

    ผม   ชื่อ จอห์น ครับ   ยินดี ที่ ได้ รู้จัก

      My name is John.   Nice to meet you.

Supa: chên-gan kâ.

สุภา: เช่นกัน   ค่ะ

(*same*) *Nice to meet you, too.*   *or not?*

      feel good

Conversation 2

Somchai: sà-baai dii rนน kráp.

สมชาย: สบาย   ดี หรือ ครับ

      How are you?

Ginny: sà-baai dii kâ. kun lâ ká.

จินนี่:   สบาย ดี ค่ะ คุณ ล่ะ คะ   *gau*

      I'm fine. How about you?

Somchai: pǒm gɔ̂ɔ sà-baai dii. kɔɔpkun kráp.

สมชาย: ผม ก็ สบาย   ดี   ขอบคุณ ครับ

      I'm also fine. Thank you.

*Note: When practicing dialogues such as those above, use the appropriate
gender particles and pronouns (kráp and pǒm for males; ká, kâ and
dì-chán or chán for females).*

bprà-yòok   ประโยค   *Sentences*

1. A: nîi năngsǔu châi mái.
       นี่ หนังสือ   ใช่ ไหม
       Is this a book?
    B: châi, nîi năngsǔu.
       ใช่ นี่ หนังสือ
       Yes, this is a book.
2. A: nân sà-mùt châi mái.
       นั่น สมุด   ใช่ ไหม
       Is that a notebook?
    B: mâi châi, nân mâi châi sà-mùt.
       ไม่ ใช่ นั่น ไม่ ใช่ สมุด
       No, that is not a notebook.
3. A: nîi à-rai.
       นี่ อะไร
       What is this?
    B: nân grà-bpǎo.
       นั่น กระเป๋า
       That is a bag.
4. A: nîi naa-lí-gaa rǔu bpàak-gaa.
       นี่ นาฬิกา   หรือ ปากกา
       Is this a watch or a pen?
    B: nân bpàak-gaa.
       นั่น ปากกา
       That is a pen.
5. A: kâo-jai mái.
       เข้าใจ ไหม
       Do you understand?
    B: kâo-jai.
       เข้าใจ
       Yes, (I understand).
    C: mâi kâo-jai.
       ไม่ เข้าใจ
       No, (I don't understand).

6. A: kɔ̌ɔ-tôot.
   ขอโทษ
   Excuse me.
   B: mâi bpenrai.
   ไม่ เป็นไร
   That's all right.
7. A: kɔ̀ɔpkun.
   ขอบคุณ
   Thank you.
   B: mâi bpenrai.
   ไม่ เป็นไร
   You're welcome.

Notes: 1. *The speaker decides whether to use the polite particle* kráp *or* kâ
   at the end of a sentence depending on the level of politeness desired.
   kráp *(for men) always keeps the same tone. For women,* ká *is*
   used when asking questions, and kâ *is used when making a*
   statement.
    e.g. Woman A: sà-baai dii mái <u>ká.</u> *(How are you?)*
      Woman B: sà-baai dii <u>kâ.</u>   *(I'm fine.)*
   2. *The subject of a sentence is often omitted when understood from*
   the context.
    e.g. A: kun sà-baai dii mái. = sà-baai dii mái. *(How are you?)*
      B: pǒm sà-baai dii. = sà-baai dii. *(I'm fine.)*
   3. *Thai has no direct "yes" or "no". We simply repeat the main*
   verb or adjective used in the question.
    e.g. A: kâo-jai mái. *(Understand?)*
      B: kâo-jai. *(Understand.)*
      C: mâi kâo-jai. *(Not understand.)*
    *Be careful not to use "*châi*" for "yes" and "*mâi châi*" for "no"*
   *all the time. Use them primarily when the question is "*châi mái*".*
   4. *The text does not use polite articles at the end of the sentences*
   in the practice sentence sections. You can add them in the appropriate
   gender by yourself. Your speech may seem rude and abrupt without
   a liberal sprinkling of polite particles, but you don't need to use them
   after every sentence.

jamnuan จำนวน *Numbers*

0	sǔun *soon*	ศูนย์
1	nùng	หนึ่ง
2	sɔ̌ɔng *soug*	สอง
3	sǎam	สาม
4	sìi *see*	สี่
5	hâa	ห้า
6	hòk	หก
7	jèt	เจ็ด
8	bpὲὲt *bat*	แปด
9	gâao	เก้า
10	sìp	สิบ
11	sìp-èt	สิบเอ็ด
12	sìpsɔ̌ɔng	สิบสอง
13	sìpsǎam	สิบสาม
20	yîi-sìp	ยี่สิบ
21	yîi-sìp-èt	ยี่สิบเอ็ด
22	yîi-sìpsɔ̌ɔng	ยี่สิบสอง
30	sǎamsìp	สามสิบ
31	sǎamsìp-èt	สามสิบเอ็ด
32	sǎamsìpsɔ̌ɔng	สามสิบสอง
40	sìi-sìp	สี่สิบ
50	hâa-sìp	ห้าสิบ
60	hòksìp	หกสิบ
70	jètsìp	เจ็ดสิบ
80	bpὲὲtsìp	แปดสิบ
90	gâao-sìp	เก้าสิบ
100	(nùng) rɔ́ɔi *roy*	(หนึ่ง) ร้อย
200	sɔ̌ɔngrɔ́ɔi	สองร้อย
300	sǎamrɔ́ɔi	สามร้อย

1,000	(nùng) pan	(หนึ่ง) พัน
2,000	sɔ̌ɔngpan	สองพัน
3,000	sǎampan	สามพัน
10,000	(nùng) mùun	(หนึ่ง) หมื่น
100,000	(nùng) sɛ̌ɛn	(หนึ่ง) แสน
1,000,000	(nùng) láan	(หนึ่ง) ล้าน
10,000,000	sìp láan	สิบล้าน
100,000,000	(nùng) rɔ́ɔi láan	(หนึ่ง) ร้อยล้าน
1,000,000,000	(nùng) pan láan	(หนึ่ง) พันล้าน
10,000,000,000	(nùng) mùun láan	(หนึ่ง) หมื่นล้าน
100,000,000,000	(nùng) sɛ̌ɛn láan	(หนึ่ง) แสนล้าน
1,000,000,000,000	(nùng) láan láan	(หนึ่ง) ล้านล้าน

1.3	nùng jùt sǎam	หนึ่งจุดสาม
2 3/5	sɔ̌ɔng sèet sǎam sùan hâa	สองเศษสามส่วนห้า
4^2	sìi gamlang sɔ̌ɔng	สี่กำลังสอง

Notes: 1. *For ordinal numbers, add* tîi (ที่) *in front of cardinal numbers.*

    e.g.   tîi nùng (ที่หนึ่ง) = the first
             tîi sɔ̌ɔng (ที่สอง) = the second
             tîi sǎam (ที่สาม) = the third
             tîi sìp (ที่สิบ)   = the tenth

  2. *For telephone numbers, 2 is sometimes pronounced as* too (โท).
    e.g. 326-9452 *is read as* sǎam-too-hòk-gâao-sìi-hâa-too

Test 1

Match the English words with the Thai words.

_____	1. *watch*	a. à-rai อะไร
_____	2. *book*	b. bpàakgaa ปากกา
_____	3. *pen*	c. nîi นี่
_____	4. *this*	d. dì-chán ดิฉัน
_____	5. *I (male speaker)*	e. naa-lí-gaa นาฬิกา
_____	6. *also*	f. nân นั่น
_____	7. *map*	g. pǒm ผม
_____	8. *name*	h. chûu ชื่อ
_____	9. *what*	i. grà-bpǎo กระเป๋า
_____	10. *bag*	j. nǎngsǔu หนังสือ
		k. pěɛntîi แผนที่
		l. gɔ̂ɔ ก็

Translate the following into English.

1. kun sà-baai dii mái.   คุณ สบาย ดี ไหม

    _____

2. kâo-jai mái.   เข้าใจ ไหม

    _____

3. nîi nǎngsǔu-pim châi mái.   นี่ หนังสือพิมพ์ ใช่ไหม

    _____

4. kun chûu à-rai.   คุณ ชื่อ อะไร

    _____

5. nân pěɛntîi rǔu dinsɔ̌ɔ.   นี่ แผนที่ หรือ ดินสอ

    _____

The Thai Writing System

Thai uses an alphabet of 44 consonants, 32 vowels, four tone marks and various other symbols for punctuation, numbers etc. Although there are irregular pronunciations, Thai is generally phonetic. It is pronounced the way it is written.

Learning to read and write Thai from the beginning has many advantages. Due to the fact that it is phonetic, you will be reinforcing your listening and speaking skills while learning to read and write. In fact, most people find that their pronunciation is more accurate when reading Thai script. Unlike many transliteration systems, it incorporates all the elements of pronunciation— including tones and vowel length.

The longer you rely on transliteration, the more time you waste reinforcing a writing system that will be virtually useless in Thailand. Furthermore, transliteration is a confusing hodgepodge with almost as many systems as there are books about Thailand. Put a little extra effort into learning the alphabet now! Then you can use Thai script while studying conversation, reinforcing reading and writing skills that will be invaluable to you in Thailand.

Consonant Classes

Thai consonants are divided into three classes— high, middle and low. Since it is one of the critical factors in determining a syllable's tone, you must know the consonant class in order to correctly pronounce what you have read.

The names (high, middle and low) of the consonant classes are completely arbitrary. For example, a low consonant may generate a high tone and a high consonant can generate a low tone, etc.

What Determines the Tone

1.   Consonant class: whether the initial consonant is high, middle or low.

2.   Vowel length: whether short or long.

3.   Tone Mark: whether or not there is a tone mark placed above the initial consonant of a syllable. (If the consonant has a superscript vowel, the tone mark is placed above that vowel.)

4.   Final consonant: whether sonorant final or stop final.

Middle Consonants (อักษรกลาง)

There are nine "middle" consonants in Thai as follows:

Consonant	Consonant Name	Sound
ก	ก ไก่ gɔɔ gài *(chicken)*	/g/
จ	จ จาน jɔɔ jaan *(plate)*	/j/
ฎ	ฎ ชะฎา dɔɔ chá-daa *(a kind of crown)*	/d/
ฏ	ฏ ปะฏัก dtɔɔ bpà-dtàk *(a kind of spear)*	/dt/
ด	ด เด็ก dɔɔ dèk *(child)*	/d/
ต	ต เต่า dtɔɔ dtào *(turtle)*	/dt/
บ	บ ใบไม้ bɔɔ bai-máai *(leaf)*	/b/
ป	ป ปลา bpɔɔ bplaa *(fish)*	/bp/
อ	อ อ่าง ɔɔ àang *(basin)*	/silent/

Note: ฎ *and* ฏ *are rare.*

Practice Writing the Middle Consonants

All the middle consonants are written with one stroke starting near the **❶**. Notice that you always start with the small circle where there is one.

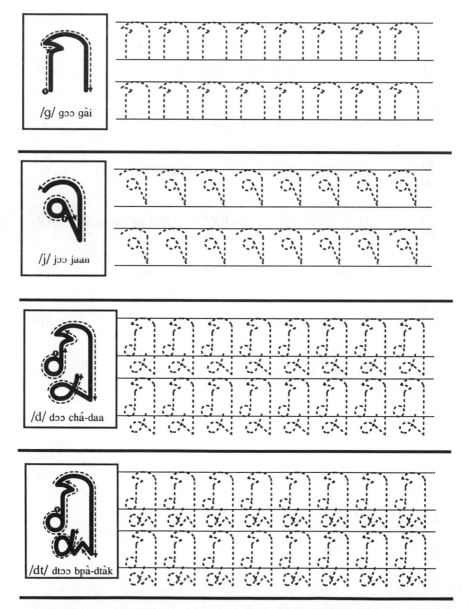

/g/ gɔɔ gài

/j/ jɔɔ jaan

/d/ dɔɔ chá-daa

/dt/ dtɔɔ bpà-dtàk

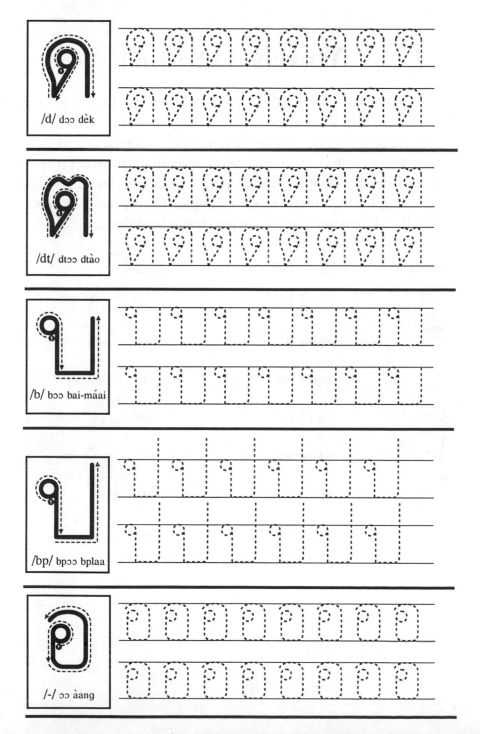

/d/ dɔɔ dèk

/dt/ dtɔɔ dtào

/b/ bɔɔ bai-máai

/bp/ bpɔɔ bplaa

/-/ ɔɔ àang

Vowels สระ (sà-rà)

Thai has two kinds of vowels: short and long. In this lesson we will learn the following **long vowels**. Every Thai syllable starts with a consonant (even if the consonant is a silent อ /-/) . Although the consonant sound comes first, the vowel may be written before, above, below, after or around the consonant depending on the vowel. In the examples below, the dash represents the place where the consonant should be written.

Vowel	Vowel Name	Sound	
-า	sà-rà aa	/aa/	a ⇒ father
◌ี	sà-rà ii	/ii/	e ⇒ see
◌ู	sà-rà uu	/uu/	u ⇒ ruler
เ-	sà-rà ee	/ee/	a as in pale
โ-	sà-rà oo	/oo/	o ⇒ go
ไ-	sà-rà ai	/ai/	
เ-า	sà-rà ao	/ao/	

Practice Writing the Following Vowels

Use อ /-/ as the consonant when practicing the following vowels. Always start with the small circle where there is one.

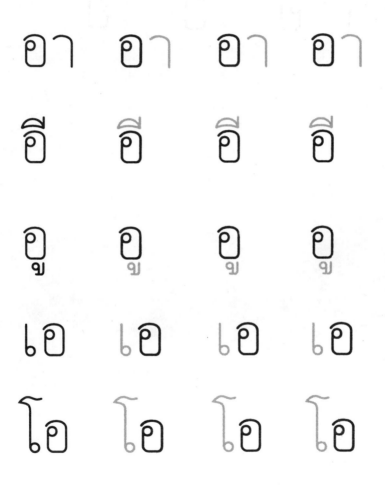

ไอ   ไอ   ไอ   ไอ

เอา   เอา   เอา   เอา

Read The Following Aloud

1.	กา	กี	กู	เก	โก	ไก	เกา
2.	จา	จี	จู	เจ	โจ	ไจ	เจา
3.	คา	คี	คู	เค	โค	ไค	เคา
4.	ตา	ตี	ตู	เต	โต	ไต	เตา
5.	บา	บี	บู	เบ	โบ	ไบ	เบา
6.	ปา	ปี	ปู	เป	โป	ไป	เปา
7.	อา	อี	อู	เอ	โอ	ไอ	เอา

<u>Tone Marks (Thai Script)</u>

Thai has four tone marks. When a tone mark is used, it is always placed above the initial consonant of the syllable. If the consonant has a superscript vowel, the tone mark is placed above that vowel.

<u>Tone Mark</u>	<u>Name</u>
่	mái èek (ไม้เอก)
้	mái too (ไม้โท)
๊	mái dtrii (ไม้ตรี)
๋	mái jàt-dtà-waa (ไม้จัตวา)

Tone Marks With Middle Consonants

With middle consonant syllables, all five tones are possible and all four tone marks can be used.

Tone Mark	Tone Name	Tone	Examples
None	sǐang sǎa-man	*mid*	กา (gaa)
่	sǐang èek	*low*	ก่า (gàa)
้	sǐang too	*falling*	ก้า (gâa)
๊	sǐang dtrii	*high*	ก๊า (gáa)
๋	sǐang jàt-dtà-waa	*rising*	ก๋า (gǎa)

Read The Following Aloud

1. กา   ก่า   ก้า   ก๊า   ก๋า
2. กี   กี่   กี้   กี๊   กี๋
3. กู   กู่   กู้   กู๊   กู๋
4. เก   เก่   เก้   เก๊   เก๋
5. โก   โก่   โก้   โก๊   โก๋
6. ไก   ไก่   ไก้   ไก๊   ไก๋
7. เกา   เก่า   เก้า   เก๊า   เก๋า

8.　จี　จี่　จี้　จี๊　จี๋

9.　จู　จู่　จู้　จู๊　จู๋

10.　เจ　เจ่　เจ้　เจ๊　เจ๋

11.　โจ　โจ่　โจ้　โจ๊　โจ๋

12.　ไจ　ไจ่　ไจ้　ไจ๊　ไจ๋

13.　เจา　เจ่า　เจ้า　เจ๊า　เจ๋า

14.　คู　คู่　คู้　คู๊　คู๋

15.　เค　เค่　เค้　เค๊　เค๋

16.　โค　โค่　โค้　โค๊　โค๋

17.　ไค　ไค่　ไค้　ไค๊　ไค๋

18.　เคา　เค่า　เค้า　เค๊า　เค๋า

19.　เต　เต่　เต้　เต๊　เต๋

20.　โต　โต่　โต้　โต๊　โต๋

21.　ไต　ไต่　ไต้　ไต๊　ไต๋

22.　เตา　เต่า　เต้า　เต๊า　เต๋า

23.　โบ　โบ่　โบ้　โบ๊　โบ๋

24.　ไบ　ไบ่　ไบ้　ไบ๊　ไบ๋

25.　เบา　เบ่า　เบ้า　เบ๊า　เบ๋า

26.　ไป　ไป่　ไป้　ไป๊　ไป๋

27.　เปา　เป่า　เป้า　เป๊า　เป๋า

28.　เอา　เอ่า　เอ้า　เอ๊า　เอ๋า

Writing Exercise 1

Transcribe the following into Thai script. Use ด and ต for the /d/ and /dt/ sounds respectively.

1. daa _____   11. jai _____

2. gǒo _____   12. dtào _____

3. bâi _____   13. oo _____

4. dtùu _____   14. bpai _____

5. ao _____   15. gúu _____

6. bpǒo_____   16. bǒo _____

7. gào _____   17. jǎa _____

8. jîi _____   18. dao _____

9. âi _____   19. gìi _____

10. bée _____   20. áa _____

Lesson 2

'bpen', 'yùu' (to be); more vowels; live and dead syllables; tone rules for middle consonants

bòtȟii sɔ̌ɔng   บทที่ ๒   *Lesson 2*

kamsàp   คำศัพท์   *Vocabulary*

too-rá-sàp โทรศัพท์		*telephone*
too-rá-tát/tii-wii โทรทัศน์/ ทีวี		*television*
wên-dtaa แว่นตา		*eye-glasses*
ngən เงิน *ng aun*		*money*
dìk/pótjà-naa-nú-grom		*dictionary*
ดิก/ พจนานุกรม		
rûup/rûup-pâap รูป/รูปภาพ		*picture*
grà-dàat กระดาษ		*paper*
dtó โต๊ะ		*table*
gâo-îi เก้าอี้		*chair*
hɔ̂ng ห้อง		*room*
hɔ̂ng-nɔɔn ห้องนอน *hong nohn*		*bedroom*
hɔ̂ng-náam ห้องน้ำ		*bathroom*
bâan บ้าน		*house*
bpen เป็น		*to be something*
yùu อยู่		*to be somewhere (live, stay)*
ao เอา		*to get, take, want*
nai ใน		*in*
bon บน		*on*
dtâai ใต้ *die*		*under*
rá-wàang ระหว่าง		*between*
gàp กับ		*and, with*
mâi dâai ไม่ได้		*not*
mʉang เมือง		*town, city*
kon คน		*person*

kon tai คนไทย	*Thai*
kon laao คนลาว	*Laotian*
kon jiin คนจีน	*Chinese*
kon yîi-bpùn คนญี่ปุ่น	*Japanese*
kon à-mee-rí-gaa คนอเมริกา	*American*
kon fà-ràngsèet คนฝรั่งเศส	*Frenchman*
kon gao-lǐi คนเกาหลี	*Korean*
kon ang-grìt คนอังกฤษ	*Englishman*
kon kǎai คนขาย	*vendor*
bprà-têet ประเทศ	*country*
bprà-têet tai/mɯang tai	*Thailand*
ประเทศไทย/เมืองไทย	
bprà-têet jiin ประเทศจีน	*China*
bprà-têet yîi-bpùn ประเทศญี่ปุ่น	*Japan*
bprà-têet à-mee-rí-gaa	*America*
ประเทศอเมริกา	
bprà-têet ang-grìt ประเทศอังกฤษ	*England*
paa-sǎa ภาษา	*language*
paa-sǎa tai ภาษาไทย	*Thai language*
paa-sǎa ang-grìt ภาษาอังกฤษ	*English language*
tîi ที่	*at*
tîi-nîi ที่นี่	*(over) here*
tîi-nân ที่นั่น	*(over) there*
tîi-nôon ที่โน่น	*(over) there (further)*
tîi-nǎi ที่ไหน	*where*
taang ทาง	*way*
sáai ซ้าย	*left*
kwǎa ขวา	*right*
níi นี้	*this[1]*
nán นั้น	*that[1]*

nóon โน้น	*that (further away)[1]*
an níi อันนี้	*this one*
an nán อันนั้น	*that one*
an nóon อันโน้น	*that one (further away)*
an nǎi อันไหน	*which one*
tâo-rài เท่าไหร่	*how much[2]*
gìi กี่	*how many[2]*
bàat บาท	*baht*
dɔɔk/dɔɔnlâa ดอล/ดอลล่าร์	*dollar*
yeen เยน	*yen*
tùuk ถูก	*cheap*
pɛɛng แพง	*expensive*
yâak ยาก	*difficult*
ngâai ง่าย	*easy*
mâak มาก	*very, many*
rao/pûak rao เรา/พวกเรา	*we, us*
káo เขา (เค้า)	*he, she, him, her*
pûak káo พวกเขา (พวกเค้า)	*they, them*
man มัน	*it*

1. níi, nán nôon *are pronouns which can stand alone.*
   níi, nán nóon *are adjectives which modify classifiers.*
   e.g. 1. níi tâo-rài. = *How much is this?*
   2. anníi tâo-rai. = *How much is this one?*

2. *You use* tâo-rài (เท่าไหร่) *, which means "how much", without a classifier when asking about the quantity of uncountable nouns. But* gìi (กี่) *which means "how many" must be followed by a classifier.*
   e.g. 1. anníi tâo-rai. = *How much is this one?*
   2. anníi gìi bàat. = *How many baht is this one?*

Conversation 1

Lek: dì-chán bpen kon tai kâ. kun bpen kon à-rai ká.

เล็ก: ดิฉัน เป็น คน ไทย ค่ะ คุณ เป็น คน อะไร คะ

I'm Thai. What nationality are you?

Tony: pǒm bpen kon à-mee-rí-gan kráp.

โทนี่: ผม เป็น คน อเมริกัน ครับ

I'm American.

Lek: kun yùu tîi-nǎi ká.

เล็ก: คุณ อยู่ ที่ไหน คะ

Where do you live?

Tony: pǒm yùu tîi saanfraan kráp.

โทนี่: ผม อยู่ ที่ ซานฟราน ครับ

I live in San Francisco.

kun lâ kráp.

คุณ ล่ะ ครับ

And you?

Lek: yùu tîi grung-têep kâ.

เล็ก: อยู่ ที่ กรุงเทพ ค่ะ

I live in Bangkok.

Notes: 1. kon à-mee-rí-gaa *or* kon à-mee-rí-gan = *American*
2. grung-têep = *Bangkok*
3. yùu tîi grung-têep *literally means 'I live at Bangkok'.*

Conversation 2

Jim: an níi tâo-rài kráp.

จิม: อัน นี้ เท่าไหร่ ครับ

     How much is this one?

Konkǎai: sìi-sìp bàat kâ.

คนขาย: สี่สิบ บาท ค่ะ

     Forty baht.

Jim: pɛɛng mâak.

จิม: แพง มาก

     That's very expensive.

     an nán gìi bàat kráp.

     อัน นั้น กี่ บาท ครับ

     How much is that one?

Konkǎai: sǎam-sìp bàat kâ.

คนขาย: สามสิบ บาท ค่ะ

     Thirty baht.

Jim: mâi pɛɛng. pǒm ao an níi.

จิม: ไม่ แพง ผม เอา อัน นี้

     That's not expensive. I take this one.

Konkǎai: kɔɔpkun mâak kâ.

คนขาย: ขอบคุณ มาก ค่ะ

     Thank you very much.

Jim: mâi bpenrai kráp.

จิม: ไม่ เป็นไร ครับ

     You're welcome.

bprà-yòok   ประโยค   *Sentences*

1. A: too-rá-sàp yùu tîi-nǎi.
    โทรศัพท์ อยู่ ที่ไหน
    Where is the phone?

    B: too-rá-sàp yùu bon dtó.
    โทรศัพท์ อยู่ บน โต๊ะ
    The phone is on the table.

    A: kun yùu tîi-nǎi.
    คุณ อยู่ ที่ไหน
    Where are you?

    B: pǒm yùu tîi bâan.
    ผม อยู่ ที่ บ้าน
    I'm at home.

    A: káo yùu tîi-nǎi.
    เขา อยู่ ที่ไหน
    Where is he?

    B: káo yùu tîi-nîi.
    เขา อยู่ ที่นี่
    He is here.

    A: hông-náam yùu tîi-nǎi.
    ห้องน้ำ   อยู่ ที่ไหน
    Where is the bathroom?

    B: hông-náam yùu taang sáai.
    ห้องน้ำ   อยู่ ทาง ซ้าย
    The bathroom is on the left.

2. A: kun bpen kon à-rai.
    คุณ เป็น คน อะไร
    What nationality are you?

    B: dì-chán bpen kon à-mee-rí-gan.
    ดิฉัน   เป็น คน อเมริกัน
    I am American.

    A: káo bpen kon à-rai.
    เขา เป็น คน อะไร
    What nationality is he?

B: káo bpen kon tai.
เขา เป็น คน ไทย
He is Thai.

A: kun taa-naa-kà bpen kon à-rai.
คุณ ทานากะ เป็น คน อะไร
What nationality is Mrs. Tanaka?

B: káo bpen kon yîi-bpùn.
เขา เป็น คน ญี่ปุ่น
She is Japanese.

3. A: an níi tâo-rài.
อัน นี้ เท่าไหร่
How much is this one?

   B: an níi 50 bàat.
อัน นี้ 50 บาท
This one is 50 baht.

   A: an nóon tâo-rài.
อัน โน้น เท่าไหร่
How much is that one over there?

   B: 2,000 yeen.
2,000 เยน
2,000 yen.

   A: nân tâo-rài.
นั่น เท่าไหร่
How much is that?

   B: níi 6 dɔɔn (lâa).
นี่ 6 ดอล (ล่าร์)
This is 6 dollars.

4. A: too-rá-sàp yùu bon dtó châi mái.
โทรศัพท์ อยู่ บน โต๊ะ ใช่ ไหม
Is the phone on the table?

   B: châi, too-rá-sàp yùu bon dtó.
ใช่ โทรศัพท์ อยู่ บน โต๊ะ
Yes, the phone is on the table.

   C: mâi châi, too-rá-sàp mâi dâai yùu bon dtó.
ไม่ ใช่ โทรศัพท์ ไม่ ได้ อยู่ บน โต๊ะ
No, the phone is not on the table.

5. A: pûak káo bpen kon yîi-bpùn ~~rǔu~~ kon gao-lǐi.
    พวก เขา เป็น คน   ญี่ปุ่น หรือ คน เกาหลี
    Are they Japanese or Korean?

    B: pûak káo bpen kon gao-lǐi.
    พวก เขา เป็น คน เกาหลี
    They are Korean.

6. A: kun bpen kon tai châi mái.
    คุณ เป็น คน ไทย ใช่ ไหม
    Are you Thai?

    B: châi, pǒm bpen kon tai.
    ใช่ ผม เป็น คน ไทย
    Yes, I'm Thai.

    C: mâi châi, pǒm bpen kon laao.
    ไม่ ใช่ ผม เป็น คน ลาว
    No, I'm Laotian.

7. A: paa-sǎa tai yâak mái.
    ภาษา ไทย ยาก ไหม
    Is Thai difficult?

    B: yâak.
    ยาก
    Yes. (Difficult)

    C: mâi yâak.
    ไม่ ยาก
    No. (Not difficult)

8. A: paa-sǎa tai ngâai.
    ภาษา ไทย ง่าย
    Thai is easy.

    B: paa-sǎa tai mâi ngâai.
    ภาษา ไทย ไม่ ง่าย
    Thai is not easy.

    C: paa-sǎa ang-grìt yâak.
    ภาษา อังกฤษ ยาก
    English is difficult.

    D: paa-sǎa ang-grìt mâi yâak.
    ภาษา อังกฤษ ไม่ ยาก
    English is not difficult.

9. A: an níi pɛɛng.
   อัน นี้ แพง
   This one is expensive.

   B: an níi mâi pɛɛng.
   อัน นี้ ไม่ แพง
   This one is not expensive.

10. nǎngsǔu yùu rá-wàang dtó gàp gâo-îi.
    หนังสือ อยู่ ระหว่าง โต๊ะ กับ เก้าอี้
    The book is between the table and the chair.

Notes: 1. 'kun' *means* "you", *and it is placed in front of people's first names to address them in a polite way.*

2. 'mâi-dâai' *is a negative form like 'not' in English, and is used with verbs. It also means 'cannot' (see lesson 3) and 'did not' (see lesson 7).*
   e.g. nǎngsǔu <u>mâi dâai</u> yùu bon dtó.
   (The book is not on the table.)
   pǒm <u>mâi dâai</u> bpen kon yîi-bpùn. *(I'm not Japanese.)*

3. mâi châi *is a negative form like 'no' or 'not', and is used with nouns.*
   e.g. pǒm <u>mâi-châi</u> kon yîi-bpùn. *(I'm not Japanese.)*

4. *There is no exact 'yes' or 'no' in Thai. To answer 'yes', simply repeat the verb or the adjective used in the question. To answer 'no', put* mâi *before the appropriate word (see sentence number 7).*

Test 2

Match the English words with the Thai words.

_____ 1. *chair*   a. too-rá-sàp โทรศัพท์

_____ 2. *table*   b. dtâai ใต้

_____ 3. *money*   c. din-sɔ̌ɔ ดินสอ

_____ 4. *Thai people*   d. káo เขา

_____ 5. *Japanese*   e. kon ang-grìt คนอังกฤษ

_____ 6. *Englishman*   f. pɛɛng แพง

_____ 7. *in*   g. bon บน

_____ 8. *on*   h. yâak ยาก

_____ 9. *under*   i. mʉang เมือง

_____ 10. *telephone*   j. hɔ̂ng-nɔɔn ห้องนอน

_____ 11. *bedroom*   k. dtó โต๊ะ

_____ 12. *television*   l. kon tai คนไทย

_____ 13. *he/she*   m. gâo- îi เก้าอี้

_____ 14. *expensive*   n. ngən เงิน

_____ 15. *difficult*   o. kon yîi-bpùn คนญี่ปุ่น

                           p. nai ใน

                           q. too-rá-tát โทรทัศน์

                           r. tùuk ถูก

Translate the following into English.

1. too-rá-sàp yùu bon gâo-îi.

   โทรศัพท์ อยู่ บน เก้าอี้

   _____

2. káo bpen kon jiin, mâi châi kon yîi-bpùn.

   เขา เป็น คน จีน ไม่ ใช่ คน ญี่ปุ่น

   _____

3. an níi tâo-rài.

   อัน นี้ เท่าไหร่

   _____

4. hɔ̂ng-náam yùu tîi-nǎi.

   ห้องน้ำ อยู่ ที่ไหน

   _____

5. paa-sǎa ang-grìt yâak mâak.

   ภาษา อังกฤษ ยาก มาก

   _____

More Vowels สระ (sà-rà)

The long vowels below include those from lesson one plus five more. Each has a corresponding short vowel form. The difference between a short and long vowel is an important one— it can change a word's meaning by itself. Also, the tone rules for short and long vowels are different.

	Short Vowel		Long Vowel	
1.	− ะ /à/	− า /aa/	father
2.	− ิ /ì/	− ี /ii/	see
3.	− ึ /ʉ̀/	− ือ /ʉʉ/	rug
4.	− ุ /ù/	− ู /uu/	ruler
5.	เ−ะ /è/	เ− /ee/	pale
6.	แ−ะ /ὲ/	แ− /ɛɛ/	sad
7.	โ−ะ /ò/	โ− /oo/	go
8.	เ−าะ /ɔ̀/	−อ /ɔɔ/	law

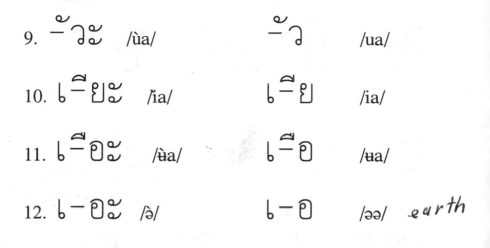

9. –ัวะ /ùa/   –ัว /ua/

10. เ–ียะ /ĭa/   เ–ีย /ia/

11. เ–ือะ /ŭa/   เ–ือ /ua/

12. เ–อะ /ə̆/   เ–อ /əə/ *earth*

Practice Writing the Following Vowels

Use อ /-/ as the consonant when practicing the following vowels.

อะ   อะ   อะ   อะ

อือ   อือ   อือ   อือ

อือ   อือ   อือ   อือ

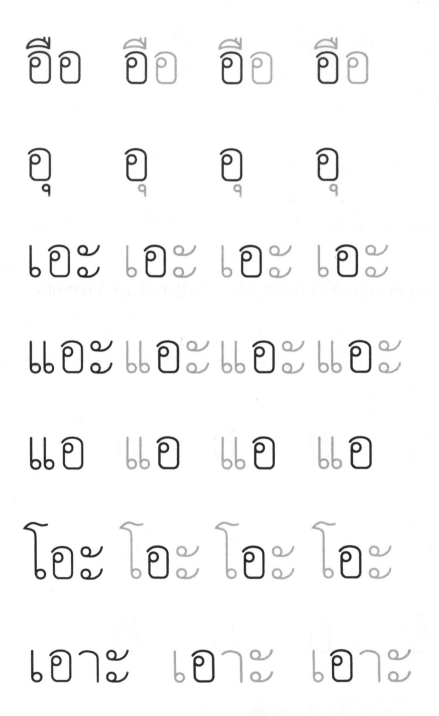

ออ ออ ออ ออ

อัวะ อัวะ อัวะ อัวะ

อัว อัว อัว อัว

เอียะ เอียะ เอียะ

เอีย เอีย เอีย

เอือะ เอือะ เอือะ

เอือ เอือ เอือ

เออะ   เออะ   เออะ

เออ   เออ   เออ

Read The Following Aloud

1.	กะ	กา	จะ	จา
2.	กิ	กี	ดิ	ดี
3.	กึ	กือ	ตึ	ตือ
4.	กุ	กู	บุ	บู
5.	เกะ	เก	เปะ	เป
6.	แกะ	แก	แอะ	แอ
7.	โกะ	โก	โจะ	โจ
8.	เกาะ	กอ	เดาะ	ดอ
9.	กัวะ	กัว	ตัวะ	ตัว
10.	เกียะ	เกีย	เบียะ	เบีย
11.	เกือะ	เกือ	เบือะ	เบือ
12.	เกอะ	เกอ	เออะ	เออ

Live and Dead Syllables
(คำเป็น-คำตาย)

Every Thai syllable is pronounced with one of the five tones, whether it has a tone mark or not. When there is no tone mark, tone rules apply. In that case, the tone is determined by consonant class and whether the syllable is live or dead.

A syllable that ends with a short vowel or a stop final consonant is called a dead syllable.

A syllable that ends with a long vowel or a sonorant final consonant is called a live syllable.

For now, just consider the short and long vowels, since we haven't introduced final consonants yet.

Tone Rules for Middle Consonants

In the absence of a tone mark, the tone rules for middle consonants are as follows:

Middle Consonant with Live Syllable = Mid Tone

Middle Consonant with Dead Syllable = Low Tone

Examples:

Middle Consonant + Long Vowel = Live Syllable

	Sound Produced	Meaning
ก + −า	= กา (gaa)	*crow*
ป + ไ−	= ไป (bpai)	*to go*
ด + ◌ู	= ดู (duu)	*to watch*

Reading Exercise: <u>Read the Following Words and Practice Writing Them in Thai.</u>

1. ดี	good	2. ใจ	heart
3. ตา	eye	4. เกา	to scratch
5. อา	uncle	6. เอา	to take
7. บัว	lotus	8. เจอ	to meet
9. ปี	year	10. ปู	crab
11. ไอ	to cough	12. เตา	stove
13. จอ	screen	14. โต	big

Middle Consonant + Short Vowel = Dead Syllable

		Sound Produced	Meaning
ก +	เ–าะ	= เกาะ (gɔ̀)	island
จ +	–ะ	= จะ (jà)	will
ด +	–ุ	= ดุ (dù)	fierce

Reading Exercise: <u>Read the Following Words and Practice Writing Them in Thai.</u>

1. ติ   *to criticize*   2. จุ   *capacity*

3. เตะ   *to kick*   4. แตะ   *to touch*

5. อี   *dung*   6. ปุ   *to put in a lining*

7. เจาะ   *to drill*   8. ปะ   *to patch (cloth)*

9. เกะกะ   *disorderly*   10. เบาะ   *cushion*

Writing Exercise 2

Transcribe the following into Thai script. Use ด and ต for the /d/ and /dt/ sounds respectively.

1. baa _____

2. gὲ _____

3. bɰa _____

4. dtù _____

5. bɔɔ _____

6. jee _____

7. gì _____

8. jə̀ _____

9. ɔɔ _____

10. jùa _____

11. gɰa _____

12. dtɔɔ _____

13. ɰɰ _____

14. bpà _____

15. gɰ̀ _____

16. dtɔ̀ _____

17. əə _____

18. dò _____

19. dua _____

20. gìa _____

Lesson 3

Colors; 'jà' (future tense); 'dâai' (can); more
vowels; complex vowels; final consonants;
Seven vowels that change their forms;
tone rules for middle consonants (cont.)

bòttîi sǎam   บทที่ ๓   *Lesson 3*

kamsàp   คำศัพท์   *Vocabulary*

jà	จะ	*will*
dâai	ได้	*can*
dtɛ̀ɛ	แต่	*but*
cháa	ช้า	*slow*
cháa-cháa	ช้าๆ	*slowly*
reo	เร็ว	*quick, fast*
reo-reo	เร็วๆ	*quickly, fast*
ìik-tii	อีกที	*one more time*
tam	ทำ	*to do, to make*
chɔ̂ɔp	ชอบ	*to like*
gin/taan	กิน/ทาน	*to eat[1]*
dùum	ดื่ม	*to drink[2]*
duu	ดู	*to watch*
pûut	พูด	*to speak*
àan	อ่าน	*to read*
kǐan	เขียน	*to write*
rian	เรียน	*to study*
sɔ̌ɔn	สอน	*to teach*
tam-ngaan	ทำงาน	*to work*
nɔɔn	นอน	*to sleep*
dtùun/dtùun-nɔɔn		*to wake up*
ตื่น/ตื่นนอน		
bpai	ไป	*to go*
maa	มา	*to come*
mâi	ไม่	*not*
gèng	เก่ง	*good at*
nítnɔ̀i	นิดหน่อย	*a little*

rót/rótyon รถ/รถยนต์	*car*
wát วัด	*temple*
bòot โบสถ์	*church*
dtà-làat ตลาด	*market*
roong-rɛɛm โรงแรม	*hotel*
roong-ngaan โรงงาน	*factory*
roong-nǎng โรงหนัง	*movie theater*
roong-rian โรงเรียน	*school*
roong-pá-yaa-baan	*hospital*
โรงพยาบาล	
tá-naa-kaan ธนาคาร	*bank*
bprai-sà-nii ไปรษณีย์	*post office*
má-hǎa-wíttá-yaa-lai	*university*
มหาวิทยาลัย	
sà-nǎam-bin สนามบิน	*airport*
ráan aa-hǎan ร้านอาหาร	*restaurant*
kà-nǒm ขนม	*snack*
kɔ̌ɔngwǎan ของหวาน	*dessert*
náam น้ำ	*water*
náamkɛ̌ng น้ำแข็ง	*ice*
náamsôm น้ำส้ม	*orange juice*
gaa-fɛɛ กาแฟ	*coffee*
chaa ชา	*tea*
bia เบียร์	*beer*
kâao ข้าว	*rice*
bà-mìi/gúai-dtǐao	*noodles*
บะหมี่/ก๋วยเตี๋ยว	
aa-hǎan อาหาร	*food*
aa-hǎan tai อาหารไทย	*Thai food*
aa-hǎan fà-ràng อาหารฝรั่ง	*western food*
aa-hǎan jiin อาหารจีน	*Chinese food*

aa-hǎan yîi-bpùn	*Japanese food*
อาหารญี่ปุ่น	
kâao-cháao/ aa-hǎan-cháao	*breakfast*
ข้าวเช้า/อาหารเช้า	
kâao-tîang/aa-hǎan-tîang	*lunch*
ข้าวเที่ยง/อาหารเที่ยง	
kâao-yen/ aa-hǎan-yen	*dinner*
ข้าวเย็น/อาหารเย็น	
ginkâao/taankâao	*to have a meal[3]*
กินข้าว/ทานข้าว	
sǐi สี	*color[4]*
sǐi dam สีดำ	*black*
sǐi kǎao สีขาว	*white*
sǐi dɛɛng สีแดง	*red*
sǐi kǐao สีเขียว	*green*
sǐi fáa สีฟ้า	*light blue*
sǐi náam-ngən สีน้ำเงิน	*dark blue*
sǐi náam-dtaan สีน้ำตาล	*brown*
sǐi lǔang สีเหลือง	*yellow*
sǐi chompuu สีชมพู	*pink*
sǐi mûang สีม่วง	*purple*
sǐi sôm สีส้ม	*orange*
sǐi tao สีเทา	*grey*

1. taan (ทาน - *to eat*) *is a polite form of* gin (กิน - *to eat*).

2. *Although* dùum (ดื่ม) *means to drink, Thai people tend to use* gin (กิน) *in less formal speech for both 'eat' and 'drink'.*
   e.g. pǒm chɔ̂ɔp gin bia. = *I like to drink beer.*

3. ginkâao (กินข้าว) *or* taankâao (ทานข้าว) *literally means "to eat rice". However, Thai people use this phrase for eating any main meal.*

4. sǐi (สี) *can be omitted when it is used to modify nouns.*
   e.g. rót sǐi kǎao = rót kǎao. *(white car)*

Conversation 1

Renu: kun pûut paa-sǎa tai dâai mái ká.

เรณุ:   คุณ พูด ภาษา ไทย ได้ ไหม คะ

Can you speak Thai?

David: dâai nítnɔ̀i kráp.

เดวิด: ได้ นิดหน่อย ครับ

Yes, a little.

Renu: kun rian paa-sǎa tai t̂ii-nǎi ká.

เรณุ:   คุณ เรียน ภาษา ไทย ที่ไหน คะ

Where did you learn Thai?

David: gàp kon tai nai à-mee-ri-gaa kráp.

เดวิด: กับ คน ไทย ใน อเมริกา   ครับ

With Thai people in America.

Renu: kun pûut tai gèng mâak.

เรณุ:   คุณ พูด ไทย เก่ง มาก

You speak Thai very well.

David: kɔ̀ɔpkun kráp.

เดวิด: ขอบคุณ ครับ

Thank you.

Note: pûut paa-sǎa tai *or* pûut tai = *to speak Thai.*

Conversation 2

Mana: kun chɔ̂ɔp taan aa-hǎan tai mái kráp.

มานะ: คุณ ชอบ ทาน อาหาร ไทย ไหม ครับ

Do you like to eat Thai food?

Paul: chɔ̂ɔp mâak kráp.

ปอล: ชอบ มาก ครับ

Yes, I like it very much.

kun chɔ̂ɔp aa-hǎan fà-rang mái kráp.

คุณ ชอบ อาหาร ฝรั่ง ไหม ครับ

Do you like western food?

Mana: mâi chɔ̂ɔp kráp. pǒm chɔ̂ɔp aa-hǎan yîi-bpùn.

มานะ: ไม่ ชอบ ครับ ผม ชอบ อาหาร ญี่ปุ่น

No, I don't. I like Japanese food.

kun jà dùʉm chaa rʉ́ gaa-fɛɛ kráp.

คุณ จะ ดื่ม ชา รึ กาแฟ ครับ

Will you drink tea or coffee?

Paul: jà dùʉm gaa-fɛɛ kráp.

ปอล: จะ ดื่ม กาแฟ ครับ

I will drink coffee.

bprà-yòok   ประโยค   *Sentences*

1. A: kun (mâi) chɔ̂ɔp   aa-hǎan à-rai.
       คุณ (ไม่) ชอบ อาหาร อะไร
       What food do (don't) you like?

    B: dì-chán (mâi) chɔ̂ɔp aa-hǎan tai.
       ดิฉัน (ไม่) ชอบ อาหาร ไทย
       I (don't) like Thai food.

    A: kun (mâi) chɔ̂ɔp   sǐi à-rai.
       คุณ (ไม่) ชอบ สี อะไร
       What color do (don't) you like?

    B: dì-chán (mâi) chɔ̂ɔp sǐi kǎao.
       ดิฉัน (ไม่) ชอบ สี ขาว
       I (don't) like white.

    A: kun (mâi) chɔ̂ɔp tam à-rai.
       คุณ (ไม่) ชอบ ทำ อะไร
       What do (don't) you like to do?

    B: dì-chán (mâi) chɔ̂ɔp duu tii-wii.
       ดิฉัน (ไม่) ชอบ ดู ทีวี
       I (don't) like watching T.V.

2. A: kun chɔ̂ɔp aa-hǎan jiin mái.
       คุณ ชอบ อาหาร จีน ไหม
       Do you like Chinese food?

    B: chɔ̂ɔp.
       ชอบ
       Yes, I do.

    C: mâi chɔ̂ɔp.
       ไม่ชอบ
       No, I don't.

3. A: kun chɔ̂ɔp aa-hǎan tai rʉ́ aa-hǎan fà-ràng.
    คุณ ชอบ อาหาร ไทย รึ อาหาร ฝรั่ง
    Do you like Thai food or western food?

    B: pǒm chɔ̂ɔp aa-hǎan tai.
    ผม ชอบ อาหาร ไทย
    I like Thai food.

    A: kun chɔ̂ɔp rót sǐi kǎao rʉ́ rót sǐi dɛɛng.
    คุณ ชอบ รถ สี ขาว รึ รถ สี แดง
    Do you like white cars or red cars?

    B: pǒm chɔ̂ɔp rót sǐi dɛɛng.
    ผม ชอบ รถ สี แดง
    I like red cars.

4. A: kun àan paa-sǎa tai dâai mái.
    คุณ อ่าน ภาษา ไทย ได้ ไหม
    Can you read Thai?

    B: dâai.
    ได้
    Yes, I can.

    C: mâi dâai.
    ไม่ ได้
    No, I can't.

5. A: kun kǐan paa-sǎa tai dâai mái.
    คุณ เขียน ภาษา ไทย ได้ ไหม
    Can you write in Thai?

    B: mâi dâai. dtɛ̀ɛ àan dâai nítnɔ̀i.
    ไม่ ได้ แต่ อ่าน ได้ นิดหน่อย
    No, I can't. But I can read a little.

6. A: kun jà bpai nǎi.
    คุณ จะ ไป ไหน
    Where will you go?

    B: jà bpai ráan aa-hǎan tai.
    จะ ไป ร้าน อาหาร ไทย
    I will go to a Thai restaurant.

C: jà bpai sà-nǎambin.
จะ ไป   สนามบิน
I will go to the airport.

7. A: káo chɔ̂ɔp dùum à-rai.
เขา ชอบ   ดื่ม อะไร
What does he/she like to drink?

B: káo chɔ̂ɔp dùum gaa-fɛɛ.
เขา ชอบ   ดื่ม   กาแฟ
He/she likes to drink coffee.

C: káo chɔ̂ɔp dùum bia   tai.
เขา ชอบ   ดื่ม เบียร์ ไทย
He/she likes to drink Thai beer.

8. A: kun tam-ngaan tîi-nǎi.
คุณ ทำงาน   ที่ไหน
Where do you work?

B: pǒm tam-ngaan tîi grung-têep.
ผม   ทำงาน   ที่ กรุงเทพ
I work in Bangkok.

A: kun jà gin kâao-tîang tîi-nǎi.
คุณ จะ กิน ข้าวเที่ยง ที่ไหน
Where will you have lunch?

B: tîi ráan aa-hǎan tai.
ที่ ร้าน อาหาร ไทย
At a Thai restaurant.

9. kɔ̌ɔ-tôot. pûut cháa-cháa dâai mái.
ขอโทษ   พูด   ช้าๆ   ได้ ไหม
Excuse me. Could you speak slowly?

10. pûut ìik tii dâai mái.
พูด อีก ที ได้ ไหม
Can you say that again?

Note: nǎi (ไหน) *is a short form of* tîi-nǎi (ที่ไหน). tîi (ที่) *is often omitted in
questions.*
e.g. kun yùu tîi-nǎi. = kun yùu nǎi. *(Where are you?)*

Test 3

Match the English words with the Thai words.

_____ 1. *school*

_____ 2. *eat*

_____ 3. *airport*

_____ 4. *temple*

_____ 5. *to speak*

_____ 6. *food*

_____ 7. *black*

_____ 8. *rice*

_____ 9. *white*

_____ 10. *tea*

_____ 11. *to watch*

_____ 12. *car*

_____ 13. *to do, to make*

_____ 14. *university*

_____ 15. *snack*

a. wát   วัด

b. sǐi dam   สีดำ

c. duu   ดู

d. sǐi kǎao   สีขาว

e. rót   รถ

f. sà-nǎam-bin   สนามบิน

g. sǐi dɛɛng   สีแดง

h. tam   ทำ

i. má-hǎa-wíttá-yaa-lai
   มหาวิทยาลัย

j. roong-rian   โรงเรียน

k. kà-nǒm   ขนม

l. kâao   ข้าว

m. aa-hǎan   อาหาร

n. gin   กิน

o. àan   อ่าน

p. chaa   ชา

q. pûut   พูด

r. roong-nǎng   โรงหนัง

Translate the following into English.

1. kun tam-ngaan tîi-nǎi.

    คุณ   ทำงาน   ที่ไหน

    _____

2. pǒm chɔ̂ɔp rót sǐi fáa.

    ผม   ชอบ   รถ   สี   ฟ้า

    _____

3. kun chɔ̂ɔp aa-hǎan tai rɯ̌ɯ aa-hǎan jiin.

    คุณ   ชอบ   อาหาร   ไทย   หรือ   อาหาร   จีน

    _____

4. káo jà bpai nǎi.

    เขา   จะ   ไป   ไหน

    _____

5. kun kǐan paa-sǎa tai dâai gèng mâak.

    คุณ   เขียน   ภาษา   ไทย ได้   เก่ง   มาก

    _____

More Vowels (sàrà - สระ)

The following vowels may sound either short or long, but are categorized as long vowels for tone rule purposes.

ำ   /am/

ใ-   /ai mái-múan/

ไ-   /ai mái-má-lai/

เ-า   /ao/

ไ- and ใ- are pronounced the same. However, there are only twenty words in the Thai language in which ใ- is used. See Lesson 9 on how to use ใ- .

The following letters can be categorized as both vowels and consonants. ฤ is used the most. ฦ and ฦๅ are obsolete. Look at the Special Features Section (page 200) for usage.

ฤ   /rú/

ฤๅ   /ruu/

ฦ   /lú/

ฦๅ   /luu/

Complex Vowels (sàrà - สระ)

The following can be considered complex vowels. They are vowels followed by the sonorant consonants ย and ว .

−ายย   /aai/

เ−ียว   /iao/

−าว   /aao/

−วย   /uai/

เ−ือย   /ɯɯai/

−อย   /ɔɔi/

โ−ย   /ooi/

−ุย   /ui/

−ิว   /iu/

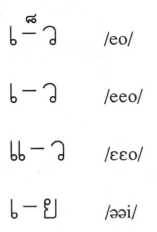

เ–ว   /eo/

เ–ว   /eeo/

แ–ว   /ɛɛo/

เ–ย   /əəi/

Practice Writing the Following Vowels

Use อ /-/ as the consonant when practicing the following vowels.

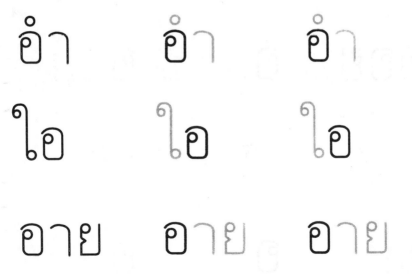

เอียว เอียว เอียว

อาว อาว อาว

อวย อวย อวย

เอือย เอือย เอือย

ออย ออย ออย

โอย โอย โอย

อุย อุย อุย

อิว   อิว   อิว

เอ็ว   เอ็ว   เอ็ว

เอว   เอว   เอว

แอว   แอว   แอว

เอย   เอย   เอย

Read The Following Aloud

1. กำ ใก ไก เกา เกย

2. จำ ใจ ไจ เจา เจย

3. ดำ ใด ได เดา เดย

4. ตำ ใต ไต เตา เตย

5. บำ ใบ ไบ เบา เบย

6. ปำ ใป ไป เปา เปย

7. อำ ใอ ไอ เอา เอย

8. กำ ก่ำ ก้ำ ก๊ำ ก๋ำ

9. ใจ ใจ่ ใจ้ ใจ๊ ใจ๋

10. ได ได่ ได้ ได๊ ได๋

11. เตา เต่า เต้า เต๊า เต๋า

12. เบย เบ่ย เบ้ย เบ๊ย เบ๋ย

Final Consonants

There are eight final consonant sounds which can end a syllable. They are divided into two categories - sonorant and stop. Sonorant finals are voiced - if you touch your larynx (voice box) while pronouncing them, you will feel a vibration. Stop finals are unvoiced. The five sonorant and three stop finals are most commonly written as follows:

Sonorant Finals

ง	ง งู	ngɔɔ nguu *(snake)*	/ng/
น	น หนู	nɔɔ nǔu *(mouse)*	/n/
ม	ม ม้า	mɔɔ máa *(horse)*	/m/
ย	ย ยักษ์	yɔɔ yák *(giant)*	/y/
ว	ว แหวน	wɔɔ wɛ̌ɛn *(ring)*	/w/

Stop Finals

ก	ก ไก่	gɔɔ gài *(chicken)*	/k/
ด	ด เด็ก	dɔɔ dèk *(child)*	/t/
บ	บ ใบไม้	bɔɔ bai-máai *(leaf)*	/p/

Notes: 1. *When* ก, ด, บ *and* ย *are initial consonants, they are transcribed as /g-/, /d-/, /b-/ and /y-/ respectively. However, when they are final consonants, they are transcribed as /-k/, /-t/, /-p/ and /-i/.*

2. *ว forms part of the vowels* ◌ัวะ *and* ◌ัว, *which are transcribed as /ùa/ and /ua/ respectively.* ◌ิว *is transcribed as /iu/ and* เ◌ียว *is transcribed as /iao/.*

Practice Writing the Following Consonants

The following consonants are written with one stroke. Start near the ❶.

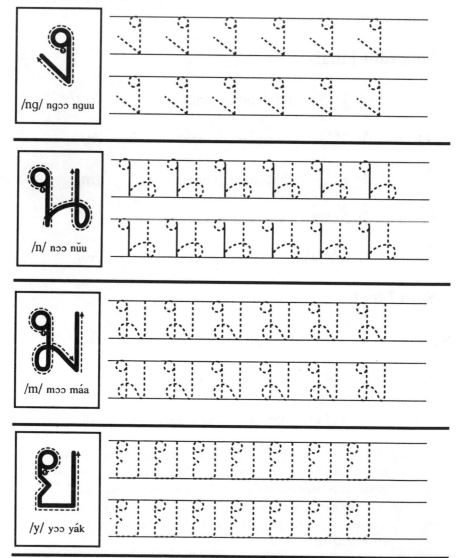

/ng/ ngɔɔ nguu

/n/ nɔɔ nǔu

/m/ mɔɔ máa

/y/ yɔɔ yák

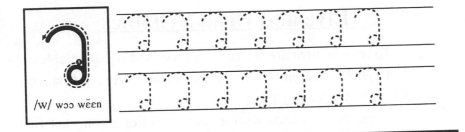

/w/ wɔɔ wɛ̌ɛn

Seven Vowels That Change Their Forms

The following seven vowels change their forms when they appear in medial position. The vowel is written differently, but the sound remains the same.

Vowels	Final Position	Medial Position
–ะ	กะ /gà/	กัด /gàt/
–ือ	ตือ /dtɯɯ/	ตืน /dtɯɯn/
เ–ะ	เปะ /bpè/	เป็น /bpen/
แ–ะ	แตะ /dtè/	แต็ก /dtèk/
โ–ะ	โจะ /jò/	จบ /jòp/
–ัว	อัว /ua/	อวน /uan/
เ–อ	เบอ /bəə/	เบิก /bə̀ək/

Live and Dead Syllables

To review, here are the rules for live and dead syllables:

A syllable that ends with a short vowel or a stop final consonant is called a <u>dead syllable</u>.

A syllable that ends with a long vowel or a sonorant final consonant is called a <u>live syllable</u>.

Rising tone and its corresponding tone mark $\left(\overset{+}{-} \right)$ never occur with a dead syllable.

Tone Rules for Middle Consonants (cont.)

In the absence of a tone mark, the tone rules for middle consonants are as follows:

Middle Consonant with <u>Live Syllable = Mid Tone</u>

Middle Consonant with <u>Dead Syllable = Low Tone</u>

Examples:

Middle Consonant + Any Vowel +<u> Sonorant Final </u>
= Live Syllable

		<u>Sound Produced</u>		<u>Meaning</u>
ก + ◌ี + น	=	กิน (gin)		*to eat*
จ + ◌ี + ง	=	จิง (jɯng)		*therefore*
ค + โ◌ + ย	=	โคย (dooi)		*by*

Middle Consonant + Any Vowel + Stop Final
  = Dead Syllable

	Sound Produced	Meaning
ก + ะ + บ	= กับ (gàp)	*with, and*
ค + โ + ค	= โคค (dòot)	*to jump*
ป + เ◌ีย + ก	= เปียก (bpìak)	*wet*

Reading Exercise: Read the Following Words and Practice Writing Them in Thai. Also Identify the Tones.

1. เอว	*waist*	2. แอบ	*to hide*
3. ตาม	*to follow*	4. จอค	*to park*
5. อาบ	*to bathe*	6. เกิน	*to exceed*
7. บน	*on*	8. ตก	*to fall*
9. ตาย	*to die*	10. จบ	*to end*
11. ปน	*to mix*	12. บุก	*to invade*
13. เตียง	*bed*	14. บาน	*to blossom*

Reading Exercise: <u>Read the Following Words and Practice Writing Them in Thai. Also Identify the Tones.</u>

1. กั้น   *to shut off*   2. ต้น   *plant*

3. ได้   *to be able to* 4. เก่า   *old*

5. ปั่น   *to spin*   6. ดิ้น   *to wriggle*

7. ปู   *grandfather*   8. ก้ม   *to bend over*

9. อิ่ม   *full*   10. จ้อง   *to stare*

11. ก้าว   *step*   12. ต้ม   *to boil*

13. บ้าน   *house*   14. ดื่ม   *to drink*

Writing Exercise 3

Transcribe the following into Thai script. Use ด and ต for the /d/ and /dt/ sounds respectively. Notice that all the vowels are in medial position and must change forms accordingly.

1. jan _____   11. don _____

2. bpɔ̀ɔt _____   12. en _____

3. bang _____   13. dɛm _____

4. guam _____   14. jɨng _____

5. jɨ̀ɨt _____   15. buam _____

6. dtem _____   16. ong _____

7. pǒm _____   17. dəən _____

8. dang _____   18. jèp _____

9. gèp _____   19. bpùat _____

10. dtòk _____   20. bùak _____

Transcribe the following into Thai script. Use ด and ต for the /d/ and /dt/ sounds respectively.

21. gân _____   31. dtǎn _____

22. jom _____   32. bìip _____

23. bâng _____   33. dâng _____

24. ùut _____   34. bàt _____

25. gûng _____   35. bàai _____

26. jaam _____   36. òong _____

27. gào _____   37. jǎa _____

28. dtʉʉn _____   38. jèp _____

29. dâam _____   39. gèɛp _____

30. ǒk _____   40. jǎao _____

Lesson 4

Telling time; high consonants; tone rules for high consonants

bòtîi sìi   บทที่ ๔   *Lesson 4*

kamsàp คำศัพท์ *Vocabulary*

wee-laa เวลา	*time*
chûa-moong ชั่วโมง	*hour*
naa-tii นาที	*minute*
wí-naa-tii วินาที	*second*
dtrong ตรง	*exactly*
krûng ครึ่ง	*half*
gùap เกือบ	*almost*
gwàa กว่า	*past*
lέεo แล้ว	*already*
bprà-maan/raao-raao	*about*
ประมาณ/ราวๆ	
ìik อีก	*more, again*
ìik hâa naa-tii อีกห้านาที	*five more minutes*
cháa ช้า	*slow*
reo เร็ว	*fast, early*
sǎai สาย	*late*
gɔ̀ɔn ก่อน	*before*
lǎng หลัง	*after*
dtɔɔn ตอน	*at*
dtɔɔn cháo ตอนเช้า	*in the morning*
dtɔɔn sǎai ตอนสาย	*late morning*
dtɔɔn tîang ตอนเที่ยง	*at noon*
dtɔɔn bàai ตอนบ่าย	*in the afternoon*
dtɔɔn yen ตอนเย็น	*in the evening*
dtɔɔn kâm ตอนค่ำ	*at night*
dtɔɔn dùk ตอนดึก	*late at night*
dtɔɔn níi/dǐao níi	*now*
ตอนนี้/เดี๋ยวนี้	

mûa-gîi-níi เมื่อกี้นี้   *just now*
mûa-rài เมื่อไหร่   *when*
jàak/dtâng-dtèɛ จาก/ตั้งแต่   *from*
tǔng ถึง   *to, until*

wee-laa เวลา *Time*

wee-laa tâo-rài   *What time is it?*
เวลาเท่าไหร่
gìi moong (léɛo)   *What time is it?*
กี่โมง (แล้ว)
gìi tûm (léɛo)   *What time is it?*
กี่ทุ่ม (แล้ว)   *(at night only)*

a.m.			
	1:00	dtii nùng	ตีหนึ่ง
	2:00	dtii sɔ̌ɔng	ตีสอง
	3:00	dtii sǎam	ตีสาม
	4:00	dtii sìi	ตีสี่
	5:00	dtii hâa	ตีห้า
	6:00	hòk moong (cháao)	หกโมง (เช้า)
	7:00	jèt moong (cháao) / (nùng) moong (cháao)
		เจ็ดโมง (เช้า)/ (หนึ่ง)โมงเช้า
	8:00	bpèɛt moong (cháao) / sɔ̌ɔng moong (cháao)
		แปดโมง (เช้า) / สองโมง (เช้า)
	9:00	gâao moong (cháao) / sǎam moong (cháao)
		เก้าโมง (เช้า) /สามโมง (เช้า)
	10:00	sìp moong (cháao) / sìi moong (cháao)
		สิบโมง (เช้า) /สี่โมง (เช้า)
	11:00	sìp-èt moong (cháao) / hâa moong (cháao)
		สิบเอ็ดโมง (เช้า) /ห้าโมง (เช้า)

p.m.	12:00	tîang/tîang-wan / dtɔɔn tîang
		เที่ยง / เที่ยงวัน / ตอนเที่ยง
	1:00	bàai nùng (moong)/ bàai moong
		บ่ายหนึ่ง (โมง) / บ่ายโมง
	2:00	(bàai) sɔ̌ɔng moong (บ่าย) สองโมง
	3:00	(bàai) sǎam moong (บ่าย) สามโมง
	4:00	(bàai) sìi moong / sìi moong yen
		(บ่าย) สี่โมง / สี่โมงเย็น
	5:00	(bàai) hâa moong / hâa moong yen
		(บ่าย) ห้าโมง / ห้าโมงเย็น
	6:00	hòk moong (yen) หกโมง (เย็น)
	7:00	(nùng) tûm (หนึ่ง) ทุ่ม
	8:00	sɔ̌ɔng tûm สองทุ่ม
	9:00	sǎam tûm สามทุ่ม
	10:00	sìi tûm สี่ทุ่ม
	11:00	hâa tûm ห้าทุ่ม
a.m.	12:00	hòk tûm/tîang-kʉʉn หกทุ่ม / เที่ยงคืน
	11:00	sìp-èt naa-lí-gaa* สิบเอ็ดนาฬิกา
	20:00	yîi-sìp naa-lí-gaa* ยี่สิบนาฬิกา
		*official

Note: There are many ways to tell time in Thai. You may not want to use them all at first. However, you will still need to understand the various forms when you hear them.

Colloquial Thai divides the 24 hour clock into four 6 hour blocks. One o'clock and seven o'clock are both one o'clock in this system; two o'clock and 8 o'clock are both 2 o'clock, etc. (this holds true for both a.m. and p.m.). The 24 hour military time system is also used, especially for official announcements (e.g. radio, train stations, airports).

Conversation

Somsak: kun dtʉ̀ʉn nɔɔn gìi moong kráp.

สมศักดิ์: คุณ ตื่น นอน กี่ โมง ครับ

   What time do you get up?

Ron: bprà-maan jèt moong kráp.

รอน: ประมาณ เจ็ด โมง ครับ

   About seven o'clock.

Somsak: gɔ̀ɔn bpai tam-ngaan kun tam à-rai.

สมศักดิ์: ก่อน ไป ทำงาน คุณ ทำ อะไร

   What do you do before going to work?

Ron: tam aa-hǎan-cháao gàp àan nǎngsʉ̌ʉ-pim.

รอน: ทำ อาหารเช้า กับ อ่าน หนังสือพิมพ์

   I make breakfast and read the paper.

Somsak: kun nɔɔn gìi tûm kráp.

สมศักดิ์: คุณ นอน กี่ ทุ่ม ครับ

   What time do you go to bed?

Ron: lǎng tiang-kʉʉn nítnɔ̀i.

รอน: หลัง เที่ยงคืน นิดหน่อย

   A little after midnight.

bprà-yòok   ประโยค   *Sentences*

1. A: dtɔɔn níi wee-laa tâo-rài.

    ตอน นี้ เวลา เท่าไหร่

    or

    dtɔɔn níi gìi moong (lέɛo).

    ตอน นี้ กี่ โมง (แล้ว)

    What time is it now?

   B: dtɔɔn níi bàai hâa moong.

    ตอน นี้ บ่าย ห้า โมง

    It's now five p.m.

   C: dtɔɔn níi tîang krûng.

    ตอน นี้ เที่ยง ครึ่ง

    It's now half past twelve noon.

   D: dtɔɔn níi gâao moong gwàa.

    ตอน นี้ เก้า โมง กว่า

    It's now a little past nine a.m.

   E: dtɔɔn níi sɔ̌ɔng moong dtrong.

    ตอน นี้ สอง โมง ตรง

    It's now exactly two p.m. (or exactly eight a.m.)

   F: dtɔɔn níi bàai sǎam sìp naa-tii.

    ตอน นี้ บ่าย สาม สิบ นาที

    It's now ten minutes after three p.m.

   G: dtɔɔn níi hâa tûm yîi-sìp.

    ตอน นี้ ห้า ทุ่ม ยี่สิบ

    It's now twenty past eleven p.m.

   H: dtɔɔn níi dtii nùng krûng.

    ตอน นี้ ตี หนึ่ง ครึ่ง

    It's now half past one a.m.

2. A: kun gin kâao-yen gìi moong.
       คุณ กิน ข้าวเย็น กี่ โมง
       What time do you eat dinner?

    B: gin kâao-yen (dtɔɔn)* hòk moong.
       กิน ข้าวเย็น (ตอน) หก โมง
       I eat dinner at six.

    A: kun bpai tam-ngaan gìi moong.
       คุณ ไป ทำงาน กี่ โมง
       What time do you go to work?

    B: bpai tam-ngaan (dtɔɔn)* bpɛ̀ɛt moong.
       ไป ทำงาน (ตอน) แปด โมง
       I go to work at eight.

    A: kun jà duu tii-wii gìi moong.
       คุณ จะ ดู ทีวี กี่ โมง
       What time will you watch T.V.?

    B: jà duu tii-wii dtɔɔn dùk.
       จะ ดู ทีวี ตอน ดึก
       I will watch T.V. late at night.
       * dtɔɔn *can be omitted in these sentences.*

3. A: hâa moong dtrong.
       ห้า โมง ตรง
       Exactly 5 p.m. (or exactly 11 a.m.)

    B: hâa moong gwàa.
       ห้า โมง กว่า
       Past 5 p.m. (or past 11 a.m.)

    C: hâa moong lɛ́ɛo.
       ห้า โมง แล้ว
       Already 5 p.m. (or already 11 a.m.)

D: bprà-maan/raao-raao hâa moong.

ประมาณ/ ราวๆ ห้า โมง

Around 5 p.m. (or around 11 a.m.)

E: gùap hâa moong.

เกือบ ห้า โมง

Almost 5 p.m. (or almost 11 a.m.)

F: ìik sìp naa-tii hâa moong.

อีก สิบ นาที ห้า โมง

Ten minutes to 5 p.m. (or ten minutes to 11 a.m.)

G: hâa moong hâa naa-tii.

ห้า โมง ห้า นาที

Five minutes past 5 p.m. (or five minutes past 11 a.m.)

H: hâa moong sìp.

ห้า โมง สิบ

Ten past 5 p.m. (or ten past 11 a.m.)

I: hâa moong krûng.

ห้า โมง ครึ่ง

Half past 5 p.m. (or half past 11 a.m.)

4. A: káo maa cháa.

เขา มา ช้า

He came slowly. (He came late.)

B: káo maa reo.

เขา มา เร็ว

He came fast. (He came early.)

C: káo maa săai.

เขา มา สาย

He came late.

5. pǒm rian paa-sǎa tai jàak bàai moong tǔng bàai sìi moong.

    ผม เรียน ภาษา ไทย จาก บ่าย โมง   ถึง   บ่าย สี่   โมง

    I study Thai from one p.m to four p.m.

6. A: kun rian paa-sǎa tai gìi chûa-moong.

    คุณ เรียน ภาษา ไทย กี่   ชั่วโมง

    How many hours do you study Thai?

    B: rao rian paa-sǎa tai sǎam chûa-moong.

    เรา เรียน ภาษา ไทย สาม   ชั่วโมง

    We study Thai for three hours.

7. A: kun àan nǎngsǔu dtâng-dtὲὲ mûa-rài.

    คุณ อ่าน หนังสือ   ตั้งแต่   เมื่อไหร่

    When did you start reading?

    B: dì-chán àan nǎngsǔu dtâng-dtὲὲ sǎam tûm.

    ดิฉัน อ่าน หนังสือ   ตั้งแต่   สาม ทุ่ม

    I've been reading since nine p.m.

    àan nǎngsǔu *literally means " to read a book". It also
    means "to read" in general.*

8. káo jà bpai sà-nǎam-bin dtɔɔn sǎam moong.

    เขา จะ ไป   สนามบิน   ตอน สาม   โมง

    He will go to the airport at three p.m. (or nine p.m.)

9. pǒm jà tam aa-hǎan tai dtɔɔn tîang.

    ผม จะ ทำ   อาหาร ไทย ตอน เที่ยง

    I will make Thai food at noon.

10. jà bpai hɔ̂ng-náam hâa naa-tii.

    จะ ไป   ห้องน้ำ   ห้า   นาที

    I will go to the bathroom for five minutes.

11. pǒm tam-ngaan hâa chûa-moong krûng.

    ผม   ทำงาน   ห้า   ชั่วโมง   ครึ่ง

    I work for five and a half hours.

12. ìik sìp naa-tii jà bpai too-rá-sàp tǔng kun.

อีก สิบ นาที จะ ไป โทรศัพท์ ถึง คุณ

I will give you a call in ten minutes.

13. dì-chan tam-ngaan jàak dtɔɔn cháao tǔng dtɔɔn tîang.

ดิฉัน ทำงาน จาก ตอน เช้า ถึง ตอน เที่ยง

I work from morning till noon.

14. A: kun jà bpai tá-naa-kaan mûa-rài.

คุณ จะ ไป ธนาคาร เมื่อไหร่

When will you go to the bank?

B: dtɔɔn bàai.

ตอน บ่าย

In the afternoon.

Test 4

Tell what time it is indicating a.m. or p.m. (Use either a.m or p.m., but if you want to write both when there is more than one answer, that's fine also.) Look at the example.

Example: săam moong =   *3:00 p.m. or 9.00 a.m.*

1. hòk moong sìphâa. หกโมงสิบห้า _____

2. săam tûm. สามทุ่ม _____

3. sìi moong krȗng. สี่โมงครึ่ง _____

4. dtii sɔ́ɔng săamsìphâa.   ตีสองสามสิบห้า

    _____

5. bàai săam moong dtrong.   บ่ายสามโมงตรง

    _____

6. ìik sìp naa-tii hâa moong.   อีกสิบนาทีห้าโมง

    _____

7. tîang yîi-sìp. เที่ยงยี่สิบ _____

8. bàai moong hâa naa-tii.   บ่ายโมงห้านาที

    _____

9. sɔ́ɔng tûm yîi-sìp naa-tii.   สองทุ่มยี่สิบนาที

    _____

10. dtii sìi.   ตีสี่ _____

11. sìi moong cháao.   สี่โมงเช้า _____

12. tîang dtrong.   เที่ยงตรง _____

13. yîi-sìp naa-lí-gaa.   ยี่สิบนาฬิกา _____

14. bpɛ̀ɛt moong sìp.   แปดโมงสิบ _____

15. hâa moong cháao.   ห้าโมงเช้า _____

Translate the following into English.

1. pǒm jà bpai wát dtɔɔn tîang.
    ผม จะ ไป   วัด ตอน เที่ยง

    _____

2. káo àan nǎngsǔu dtâng-tὲὲ hâa tûm.
    เขา อ่าน หนังสือ ตั้งแต่   ห้า ทุ่ม

    _____

3. rao rian paa-sǎa tai sǎam chûa-moong.
    เรา เรียน ภาษา ไทย สาม   ชั่วโมง

    _____

4. dtɔɔn níi wee-laa bàai moong krûng.
    ตอน นี้ เวลา   บ่าย โมง ครึ่ง

    _____

5. chán gin kâao-cháao dtɔɔn sɔ̌ɔng moong.
    ฉัน กิน ข้าวเช้า ตอน สอง โมง

    _____

High Consonants

There are eleven "high" consonants in Thai as follows:

Consonant	Consonant Name		Sound
ข	ข ไข่	kɔ̌ɔ kài (*egg*)	/k/
ฃ	ฃ ขวด	kɔ̌ɔ kùat (*bottle*)	/k/
ฉ	ฉ ฉิ่ง	chɔ̌ɔ chìng (*small cymbal*)	/ch/
ฐ	ฐ ฐาน	tɔ̌ɔ tǎan (*base*)	/t/
ถ	ถ ถุง	tɔ̌ɔ tǔng (*bag*)	/t/
ผ	ผ ผึ้ง	pɔ̌ɔ pûng (*bee*)	/p/
ฝ	ฝ ฝา	fɔ̌ɔ fǎa (*lid*)	/f/
ศ	ศ ศาลา	sɔ̌ɔ sǎa-laa (*pavilion*)	/s/
ษ	ษ ฤๅษี	sɔ̌ɔ rɯɯ-sǐi (*hermit*)	/s/
ส	ส เสือ	sɔ̌ɔ sǔa (*tiger*)	/s/
ห	ห หีบ	hɔ̌ɔ hìip (*a kind of box*)	/h/

Note: ฃ *is obsolete.*

Practice Writing the High Consonants

Notice that you always start with a small circle where there is one. Start near the ❶. ฐ, ศ, ษ, ส are written with two strokes. The remaining high consonants are written with one stroke.

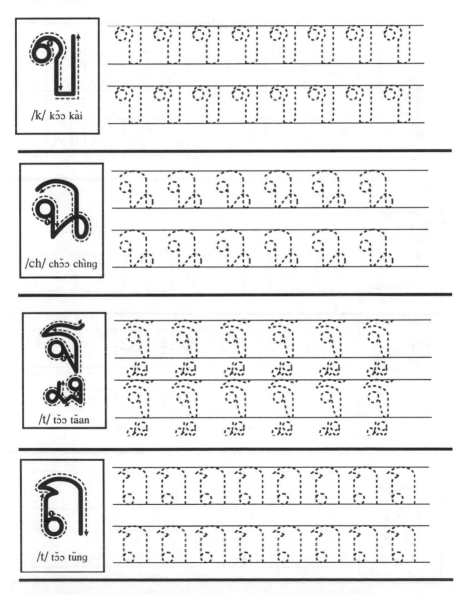

/k/ kɔ̌ɔ kài

/ch/ chɔ̌ɔ chìng

/t/ tɔ̌ɔ tǎan

/t/ tɔ̌ɔ tǔng

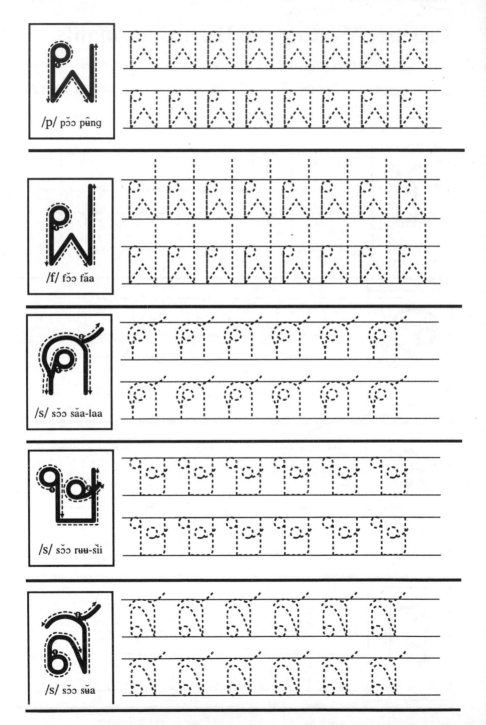

/p/ pɔ̌ɔ pʉ̂ng

/f/ fɔ̌ɔ fǎa

/s/ sɔ̌ɔ sǎa-laa

/s/ sɔ̌ɔ rʉʉ-sǐi

/s/ sɔ̌ɔ sʉ̌a

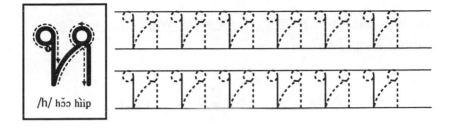

/h/ hɔ̌ɔ hìip

Tone Rules for High Consonants

In the absence of a tone mark, the tone rules for high consonants are as follows:

High Consonant with <u>Live Syllable = Rising Tone</u>

High Consonant with <u>Dead Syllable = Low Tone</u>

Examples:

High Consonant + Long Vowel = Live Syllable

	Sound Produced	Meaning
ข + −า	= ขา (kǎa)	*leg*
ผ + ◌ี	= ผี (pǐi)	*ghost*
ส + เ−า	= เสา (sǎo)	*mast*

Reading Exercise: <u>Read the Following Words and Practice Writing Them in Thai.</u>

1. หัว   *head*   2. เสือ   *tiger*

3. ไฝ   *mole*   4. หู   *ear*

5. แขน   *arm*   6. ผัว   *husband*

7. สี   *color*   8. หา   *to look for*

9. ฝา   *lid*   10. สาม   *three*

High Consonant + Short Vowel = Dead Syllable

	Sound Produced	Meaning

ห + เ–าะ   = เหาะ(hɔ̀) *to fly through the air*

ส + ◌ี   = สิ (sĭ)   *a particle used for emphasis*

Reading Exercise: <u>Read the Following Words and Practice Writing Them in Thai.</u>

1. ผุ   *rotten*   2. หี   *to chuckle*

3. แฉะ   *damp*   4. เฉาะ   *to break open*

5. เถอะ   *let's*

High Consonant + Any Vowel + <u>Sonorant Final</u>
   = Live Syllable

	<u>Sound Produced</u>	<u>Meaning</u>
ข + ◌ั + น	= ขัน (kǎn)	*bowl*
ส + –า + ม	= สาม (sǎam)	*three*
ถ + ◌ุ + ง	= ถุง (tǔng)	*sack*

High Consonant + Any Vowel + <u>Stop Final</u>
   = Dead Syllable

	<u>Sound Produced</u>	<u>Meaning</u>
ข + ◌ั + บ	= ขับ (kàp)	*to drive*
ผ + ◌ิ + ด	= ผิด (pìt)	*wrong*
ถ + ◌ู + ก	= ถูก (tùuk)	*correct*

Reading Exercise: <u>Read the Following Words and Practice</u>
<u>Writing Them in Thai. Also Identify the Tones.</u>

1. สูง   *tall*   2. ถึง   *to*

3. ฉาย   *to shine*   4. ถอด   *to take off*

5. สุก   *ripe*   6. แขก   *guest*

7. หก   *six*   8. ฐาน   *base*

9. เขย   *son-in-law*   10. สิบ   *ten*

11. ผม   *hair*   12. ขัง   *to detain*

13. สอง   *two*   14. ฝูง   *herd of animals*

Writing Exercise 4

Transcribe the following into Thai script. Use ส and ต for the initial /s/ and /t/ sounds respectively.

1. chǎa _____   11. hùp _____

2. pà _____   12. tǔng _____

3. chǎn _____   13. pǒm _____

4. kɔ̀ɔt _____   14. fǎng _____

5. sǐao _____   15. hàap _____

6. fǐi _____   16. dtè _____

7. kɛ̀ɛk _____   17. chǔn _____

8. tǐang _____   18. hǎai _____

9. fɛ̀ɛt _____   19. pàt _____

10. sɔ̌ɔn _____   20. kǎao _____

Lesson 5

Days of the week; months; tone marks with
high consonants; low consonants introduced

bòttii hâa   บทที่ ๕   *Lesson 5*

kamsàp คำศัพท์ *Vocabulary*

wan วัน	*day*
wan-aa-tít วันอาทิตย์	*Sunday*
wan-jan วันจันทร์	*Monday*
wan-angkaan วันอังคาร	*Tuesday*
wan-pút วันพุธ	*Wednesday*
wan-pá-rú-hàt (sà-bɔɔ-dii) วันพฤหัส (บดี)	*Thursday*
wan-sùk วันศุกร์	*Friday*
wan-sǎo วันเสาร์	*Saturday*
wan-yùt วันหยุด	*holiday*
sǎo-aa-tít เสาร์อาทิตย์	*weekend*
dɯan เดือน	*month*
má-gà-raa (kom) มกรา (คม)	*January[1]*
gumpaa (pan) กุมภา (พันธ์)	*February*
mii-naa (kom) มีนา (คม)	*March*
mee-sǎa (yon) เมษา (ยน)	*April*
prútsà-paa (kom) พฤษภา (คม)	*May*
mí-tù-naa (yon) มิถุนา (ยน)	*June*
gà-rá-gà-daa (kom) กรกฎา (คม)	*July*

sǐnghǎa (kom)	*August*
สิงหา (คม)	
gan-yaa (yon)	*September*
กันยา (ยน)	
dtù-laa (kom)	*October*
ตุลา (คม)	
prútsà-jì-gaa (yon)	*November*
พฤศจิกา (ยน)	
tan-waa (kom)	*December*
ธันวา (คม)	
wanníi วันนี้	*today*
mûa-waanníi เมื่อวานนี้	*yesterday*
prûng-níi พรุ่งนี้	*tomorrow*
túk ทุก	*every*
sɔ̌ɔng wan gɔ̀ɔn/sɔ̌ɔng wan tîi-lɛ́ɛo	
สองวันก่อน/ สองวันที่แล้ว	*two days ago*
sǎam wan gɔ̀ɔn/sǎam wan tîi-lɛ́ɛo	
สามวันก่อน/ สามวันที่แล้ว	*three days ago*
ìik sɔ̌ɔng wan อีกสองวัน	*two days from now*
ìik sǎam wan อีกสามวัน	*three days from now*
túk wan ทุกวัน	*everyday*
aa-tít/sàpdaa อาทิตย์/ สัปดาห์	*week[2]*
aa-tít-níi อาทิตย์นี้	*this week*
aa-tít gɔ̀ɔn/aa-tít tîi-lɛ́ɛo	*last week*
อาทิตย์ก่อน/ อาทิตย์ที่แล้ว	
aa-tít nâa อาทิตย์หน้า	*next week*

sɔ̌ɔng aa-tít gɔ̀ɔn/sɔ̌ɔng aa-tít tîi-lɛ́ɛo

สองอาทิตย์ก่อน/ สองอาทิตย์ที่แล้ว   *two weeks ago*

sǎam aa-tít gɔ̀ɔn/sǎam aa-tít tîi-lɛ́ɛo

สามอาทิตย์ก่อน/ สามอาทิตย์ที่แล้ว   *three weeks ago*

ìik sɔ̌ɔng aa-tít   อีกสองอาทิตย์   *two weeks from now*

ìik sǎam aa-tít   อีกสามอาทิตย์   *three weeks from now*

túk aa-tít   ทุกอาทิตย์   *every week*

dɯan-níi   เดือนนี้   *this month*

dɯan-tîi-lɛ́ɛo   เดือนที่แล้ว   *last month*

dɯan-nâa   เดือนหน้า   *next month*

sɔ̌ɔng dɯan gɔ̀ɔn/sɔ̌ɔng dɯan-tîi-lɛ́ɛo

สองเดือนก่อน/ สองเดือนที่แล้ว   *two months ago*

sǎam dɯan gɔ̀ɔn/sǎam dɯan tîi-lɛ́ɛo

สามเดือนก่อน/ สามเดือนที่แล้ว   *three months ago*

ìik sɔ̌ɔng dɯan   อีกสองเดือน   *two months from now*

ìik sǎam dɯan   อีกสามเดือน   *three months from now*

túk dɯan   ทุกเดือน   *every month*

bpii   ปี   *year*

bpii-níi   ปีนี้   *this year*

bpii-tîi-lɛ́ɛo   ปีที่แล้ว   *last year*

bpii-nâa   ปีหน้า   *next year*

sɔ̌ɔng bpii gɔ̀ɔn/sɔ̌ɔng bpii-tîi-lɛ́ɛo

สองปีก่อน/ สองปีที่แล้ว   *two years ago*

ìik sɔ̌ɔng bpii   อีกสองปี   *two years from now*

túk bpii   ทุกปี   *every year*

cháao   เช้า   *morning*

(mɯ̂a) cháao-níi   (เมื่อ) เช้านี้   *this morning*

prûng-níi-cháao พรุ่งนี้เช้า	*tomorrow morning*
cháao wan-aa-tít เช้าวันอาทิตย์	*Sunday morning*
túk cháao ทุกเช้า	*every morning*
yen เย็น	*evening*
yen-níi เย็นนี้	*this evening*
yen-waan-níi เย็นวานนี้	*yesterday evening*
prûng-níi-yen พรุ่งนี้เย็น	*tomorrow evening*
yen wan-aa-tít เย็นวันอาทิตย์	*Sunday evening*
túk yen ทุกเย็น	*every evening*
kʉʉn คืน	*night*
kʉʉn-níi คืนนี้	*tonight*
mʉ̂a-kʉʉn-níi เมื่อคืนนี้	*last night*
kʉʉn prûngníi คืนพรุ่งนี้	*tomorrow night*
kʉʉn wan-aa-tít คืนวันอาทิตย์	*Sunday night*
túk kʉʉn ทุกคืน	*every night*
fɛɛn แฟน	*loved one[3]*
pʉ̂an เพื่อน	*friend*
wâang ว่าง	*to have free time*
yûng ยุ่ง	*busy*
dtɔ̂ng ต้อง	*must*
mii มี	*to have, there is/are*
bplùk ปลุก	*to wake someone up*
glàp กลับ	*to return*
bpai-tîao ไปเที่ยว	*to take a trip[4]*
maa-ráp มารับ	*to come to pick up*
bpai-ráp ไปรับ	*to go to pick up*

dtὲε-cháao แต่เช้า — *early morning*

dὺk ดึก — *late at night*

săai สาย — *late*

gàp กับ — *and, together with*

bpai dûai-gan ไปด้วยกัน — *to go together*

kon diao คนเดียว — *by oneself*

mii-nát มีนัด — *have a date, appointment*

jɔɔ-gan เจอกัน — *"see you"*

hanlŏo ฮัลโหล — *"hello" (on the phone)*

oo-kee โอเค — *O.K.*

1. *The months that end with* kom (คม) *have 31 days, the months that end with* yon (ยน) *have 30 days, and February ends with* pan (พันธ์).

2. aa-tít (อาทิตย์) *means "week" and is more common than* sàpdaa (สัปดาห์) *in normal conversation. Don't get it mixed up with* wan-aa-tít (วันอาทิตย์) *which means "Sunday".*

3. fεεn (แฟน) *means loved one (e.g. boyfriend, girlfriend, husband, wife)*

4. bpai-tîao (ไปเที่ยว) *means to take a pleasure trip or to simply go out for pleasure.*

Conversation

Tim: hanlŏo.
ทิม: ฮัลโหล
         Hello.

Nit: hanlŏo. nít pûut kâ.
นิด: ฮัลโหล นิด พูด ค่ะ
         Hello. Nit speaking.

Tim: sà-wàtdii kráp kun nít. pǒm tim pûut kráp.
ทิม: สวัสดี   ครับ คุณ นิด ผม ทิม พูด ครับ
         Hi Nit. It's Tim speaking.

Nit: sà-wàtdii kâ kun tim. sà-baai dii rǔu ká.
นิด: สวัสดี   ค่ะ คุณ ทิม สบาย ดี หรือ คะ
         Hi Tim. How are you?

Tim: sà-baai dii kráp. kuun prûng-níi wâang mái kráp.
ทิม: สบาย ดี ครับ คืน   พรุ่งนี้   ว่าง ไหม ครับ
         I'm fine. Are you free tomorrow night?

Nit: mâi wâang kâ. kuun prûng-níi dtɔ̂ng tam-ngaan.
นิด: ไม่ ว่าง ค่ะ คืน   พรุ่งนี้   ต้อง ทำงาน
         No, I'm not. I have to work tomorrow night.

Tim: kuun wan-sùk lâ kráp.
ทิม: คืน   วันศุกร์ ล่ะ ครับ
         What about Friday?

Nit: kuun wan-sùk wâang kâ.
นิด: คืน   วันศุกร์ ว่าง ค่ะ
         I'm free Friday night.

Tim: pǒm jà bpai taan aa-hǎan yîi-bpùn.
ทิม: ผม จะ ไป ทาน อาหาร ญี่ปุ่น
         I will go eat out at a Japanese restaurant.

bpai duâi-gan mái kráp.

ไป ด้วยกัน ไหม ครับ

Do you want to go with me?

Nit: oo-kee kâ. kuun wan-sùk bpai dâai.

นิด: โอเค ค่ะ คืน วันศุกร์ ไป ได้

O.K. I can go Friday night.

jà bpai gìi moong ká.

จะ ไป กี่ โมง คะ

What time are you going?

Tim: bprà-maan sɔ̌ɔng tûm kráp.

ทิม: ประมาณ สอง ทุ่ม ครับ

About eight o'clock.

pǒm jà bpai-ráp dtɔɔn hòk moong krûng ná* kráp.

ผม จะ ไปรับ ตอน หก โมง ครึ่ง นะ ครับ

I will go pick you up at half past six.

Nit: kɔ̌ɔpkun kâ. jəə-gan wan-sùk dtɔɔn hòk moong krûng.

นิด: ขอบคุณ ค่ะ เจอกัน วันศุกร์ ตอน หก โมง ครึ่ง

Thank you. See you Friday at half past six.

Tim: sà-watdii kráp.

ทิม: สวัสดี ครับ

Good-bye.

Nit: sà-wàtdii kâ.

นิด: สวัสดี ค่ะ

Good-bye.

*ná (นะ) is a particle commonly used to make the statement softer and
gentler, especially if the statement is a command. For further
explanation see "Thai for Intermediate Learners".*

bprà-yòok   ประโยค   *Sentences*

1. A: wan-níi wan à-rai.
    วันนี้   วัน อะไร
    What day is today?

    B: wan-níi wan-aa-tít.
    วันนี้   วันอาทิตย์
    Today is Sunday.

2. A: prûng-níi wan à-rai.
    พรุ่งนี้   วัน อะไร
    What day is tomorrow?

    B: prûng-níi wan-jan.
    พรุ่งนี้   วันจันทร์
    Tomorrow is Monday.

3. A: dɯan-níi dɯan à-rai.
    เดือนนี้   เดือน อะไร
    What month is this?

    B: dɯan-níi dɯan mii-naa.
    เดือนนี้ เดือน มีนา
    This month is March.

4. A: bpii-níi bpii à-rai.
    ปีนี้   ปี อะไร
    What year is this?

    B: bpii-níi bpii gâao-hâa.
    ปีนี้   ปี เก้าห้า
    This year is '95.

5. A: wan-níi wan-tîi tâo-rài.
    วันนี้   วันที่ เท่าไหร่
    What is the date today?

    B: wan-níi wan-tîi sìphâa.
    วันนี้   วันที่ สิบห้า
    Today is the 15th.

C: wan-níi wan-tîi sìphâa dʉan mee-sǎa.

วันนี้ วันที่ สิบห้า เดือน เมษา

Today is April 15th.

D: wan-níi wan-sǎo tîi sìphâa dʉan mee-sǎa.

วันนี้ วันเสาร์ ที่ สิบห้า เดือน เมษา

Today is Saturday, April 15th.

6. A: kun jà bpai mʉang tai dʉan à-rai.

   คุณ จะไป เมือง ไทย เดือน อะไร

   What month are you going to Thailand?

   B: pǒm jà bpai mʉang tai dʉan gan-yaa.

   ผม จะ ไป เมือง ไทย เดือน กันยา

   I will go to Thailand in September.

7. A: kun mii wan-yùt mʉ̂a-rài.

   คุณ มี วันหยุด เมื่อไหร่

   When do you have a holiday?

   B: chán mii wan-yùt dʉan-nâa.

   ฉัน มี วันหยุด เดือนหน้า

   I have a holiday next month.

8. A: wan-aa-tít níi kun jà tam à-rai.

   วันอาทิตย์ นี้ คุณ จะ ทำ อะไร

   What will you do this coming Sunday?

   B: wan-aa-tít níi jà bpai gin aa-hǎan tai.

   วันอาทิตย์ นี้ จะ ไป กิน อาหารไทย

   This Sunday I will go to eat Thai food.

9. A: mʉ̂a-kʉʉn-níi kun tam à-rai.

   เมื่อคืนนี้ คุณ ทำ อะไร

   What did you do last night?

   B: bpai gin bia gàp pʉ̂an.

   ไป กิน เบียร์ กับ เพื่อน

   I went to drink beer with my friend.

10. A: káo yùu mɯang tai gìi bpii.
    เขา อยู่ เมือง ไทย กี่ ปี
    How long was he in Thailand?

   B: káo yùu mɯang tai hâa bpii.
    เขา อยู่ เมือง ไทย ห้า ปี
    He was in Thailand for five years.

11. A: aa-tít nâa jà tam à-rai.
    อาทิตย์ หน้า จะ ทำ อะไร
    What will you do next week?

   B: aa-tít nâa jà bpai yîi-bpùn.
    อาทิตย์ หน้า จะ ไป ญี่ปุ่น
    Next week I will go to Japan.

12.   mɯ̂a-waanníi pûut too-rá-sàp krɯ̂ng chûa-moong.
    เมื่อวานนี้ พูด โทรศัพท์ ครึ่ง ชั่วโมง
    Yesterday I talked on the phone for half an hour.

13.   pǒm rian paa-sǎa tai túk aa-tít.
    ผม เรียน ภาษา ไทย ทุก อาทิตย์
    I study Thai every week.

14.   pǒm rian paa-sǎa tai túk wan-aa-tít.
    ผม เรียน ภาษา ไทย ทุก วันอาทิตย์
    I study Thai every Sunday.

15.   káo maa tam-ngaan dtɛ̀ɛ-cháao.
    เขา มา ทำงาน แต่เช้า
    He comes to work early in the morning.

16.   sǎo-aa-tít dì-chán chɔ̂ɔp dtɯ̀ɯn sǎai.
    เสาร์อาทิตย์ ดิฉัน ชอบ ตื่น สาย
    I like to wake up late on weekends.

17. A: pûak kun yùu mɯang tai gìi dɯan.
    พวก คุณ อยู่ เมือง ไทย กี่ เดือน
    How many months were you in Thailand?

B: rao yùu mɯang tai sǎam dɯan.

เรา อยู่ เมือง ไทย สาม เดือน

We were in Thailand for three months.

18. rao yùu mɯang tai jàak mí-tù-naa tɯ̌ng sǐnghǎa.

เรา อยู่ เมือง ไทย จาก มิถุนา ถึง สิงหา

We were in Thailand from June to August.

19. káo mii wee-laa wâang túk sǎo-aa-tít.

เขา มี เวลา ว่าง ทุก เสาร์อาทิตย์

He has free time every weekend.

20. sɔ̌ɔng wan tîi-lɛ́ɛo bpai tam-ngaan sǎai.

สอง วัน ที่แล้ว ไป ทำงาน สาย

The last two days I went to work late.

21. bpii-nâa jà rian paa-sǎa tai gàp paa-sǎa jiin.

ปีหน้า จะ เรียน ภาษา ไทย กับ ภาษาจีน

Next year I will study Thai and Chinese.

22. aa-tít tîi-lɛ́ɛo glàp bâan dɯ̀k túk wan.

อาทิตย์ ที่แล้ว กลับ บ้าน ดึก ทุก วัน

Last week I returned home late everyday.

23. ìik sǎam bpii jà glàp mɯang tai.

อีก สาม ปี จะ กลับ เมือง ไทย

I will return to Thailand in three years.

24. (mɯ̂a) cháao-níi gin kâao kon diao.

(เมื่อ) เช้านี้ กิน ข้าว คน เดียว

This morning I ate breakfast by myself.

25. pǒm mii-nát gàp fɛɛn túk kɯɯn wan-sùk.

ผม มีนัด กับ แฟน ทุก คืน วันศุกร์

I have a date with my girlfriend every Friday night.

Test 5

Match the English words with the Thai words.

<u>Days</u> วัน

_____ 1. *Sunday*   a. wan-pá-rɯ́-hàt วันพฤหัส

_____ 2. *Monday*   b. wan-sǎo วันเสาร์

_____ 3. *Tuesday*   c. wan-aa-tít วันอาทิตย์

_____ 4. *Wednesday*   d. wan-sùk วันศุกร์

_____ 5. *Thursday*   e. wan-jan วันจันทร์

_____ 6. *Friday*   f. wan-angkaan วันอังคาร

_____ 7. *Saturday*   g. wan-yùt วันหยุด

_____ 8. *holiday*   h. wan-pút วันพุธ

Months เดือน

_____ 1. *January*

_____ 2. *February*

_____ 3. *March*

_____ 4. *April*

_____ 5. *May*

_____ 6. *June*

_____ 7. *July*

_____ 8. *August*

_____ 9. *September*

_____ 10. *October*

_____ 11. *November*

_____ 12. *December*

a. mee-sǎa (yon)
เมษา (ยน)

b. tan-waa (kom)
ธันวา (คม)

c. sǐnghǎa (kom)
สิงหา (คม)

d. prúsà-jì-gaa (yon)
พฤศจิกา (ยน)

e. gumpaa (pan)
กุมภา (พันธ์)

f. gan-yaa (yon)
กันยา (ยน)

g. prúsà-paa (kom)
พฤษภา (คม)

h. mí-tù-naa (yon)
มิถุนา (ยน)

i. má-gà-raa (kom)
มกรา (คม)

j. gà-rá-gà-daa (kom)
กรกฎา (คม)

k. dtù-laa (kom)
ตุลา (คม)

l. mii-naa (kom)
มีนา (คม)

<u>Tone Marks With High Consonants</u>

With high consonant syllables, there are three possible tones and two tone marks which may be used.

<u>Tone Mark</u>	<u>Tone Name</u>	<u>Tone</u>	<u>Examples</u>
่ ‒	sĭang èek	*low*	ข่า (kàa)
้ ‒	sĭang too	*falling*	ข้า (kâa)

When there is no tone mark, a high consonant syllable has either rising tone or low tone depending on whether it is a live or dead syllable. (See page 103)

Reading Exercise: <u>Read the Following Words and Practice Writing Them in Thai. Also Identify the Tones.</u>

1. สี่   *four*

2. ห่อ   *to wrap*

3. ข้าว   *rice*

4. ส้น   *heel*

5. ขั้น   *step*

6. หั่น   *to slice*

7. ผ้า   *cloth*

8. ให้   *to give*

9. ฝิ่น   *opium*

10. ถ้ำ   *cave*

11. ฉิ่ง   *cymbal*

12. ส้ม   *orange*

13. ห้า   *five*

14. เฝ้า   *to watch over*

Read The Following Aloud

1.	ข่า	ข้า	ขา	6.	ฉี่	ฉี้	ฉี	
2.	ถู่	ถู้	ถู	7.	เผ่	เผ้	เผ	
3.	ไผ่	ไผ้	ไผ	8.	เส่า	เส้า	เสา	
4.	ห่อ	ห้อ	หอ	9.	โข่	โข้	โข	
5.	แฉ่	แฉ้	แฉ	10.	ถื่อ	ถื้อ	ถือ	

Writing Exercise 5

Transcribe the following into Thai script. Use ถ and ส for the initial /t/ and /s/ sounds respectively.

1. chɔ̌i _____   11. sǔai _____

2. pûng _____   12. fàng _____

3. hûan _____   13. tìi _____

4. kǒm _____   14. fàan _____

5. pɯ̌ɯn _____   15. kǎai _____

6. tɔ̀ɔi _____   16. kâao _____

7. sòng _____   17. hɔ̌ng _____

8. kùut _____   18. fâai _____

9. pɔ̌ɔi _____   19. chàap _____

10. tǎam _____   20. sên _____

Low Consonants

There are twenty-four "low" consonants in Thai. You have seen five of them before as sonorant finals (ง, น, ม, ย, ว).

Consonant	Consonant Name		Sound
ค	ค ควาย	kɔɔ kwaai *(buffalo)*	/k/
ฅ	ฅ คน	kɔɔ kon *(person)*	/k/
ฆ	ฆ ระฆัง	kɔɔ rá-kang *(bell)*	/k/
ง	ง งู	ngɔɔ nguu *(snake)*	/ng/
ช	ช ช้าง	chɔɔ cháang *(elephant)*	/ch/
ซ	ซ โซ่	sɔɔ sôo *(chain)*	/s/
ฌ	ฌ เฌอ	chɔɔ chəə *(a kind of tree)*	/ch/
ญ	ญ หญิง	yɔɔ yǐng *(woman)*	/y/
ฑ	มณโฑ	tɔɔ montoo *(Montho the Queen)*	/t/
ฒ	ฒ ผู้เฒ่า	tɔɔ pûu-tâo *(old man)*	/t/
ณ	ณ เณร	nɔɔ neen *(young monk)*	/n/

ท	ท ทหาร	tɔɔ tá-hăan *(soldier)*	/t/
ธ	ธ ธง	tɔɔ tong *(flag)*	/t/
น	น หนู	nɔɔ nŭu *(mouse)*	/n/
พ	พ พาน	pɔɔ paan *(tray)*	/p/
ฟ	ฟ ฟัน	fɔɔ fan *(tooth)*	/f/
ภ	ภ สำเภา	pɔɔ sămpao *(a kind of ship)*	/p/
ม	ม ม้า	mɔɔ máa *(horse)*	/m/
ย	ย ยักษ์	yɔɔ yák *(giant)*	/y/
ร	ร เรือ	rɔɔ rɯa *(boat)*	/r/
ล	ล ลิง	lɔɔ ling *(monkey)*	/l/
ว	ว แหวน	wɔɔ wɛ̆ɛn *(ring)*	/w/
ฬ	ฬ จุฬา	lɔɔ jù-laa *(a kind of kite)*	/l/
ฮ	ฮ นกฮูก	hɔɔ nókhûuk (owl)	/h/

Note: ฅ *is obsolete.*

Lesson 6

'ao', 'yàak' (to want); 'gamlang' (to be ... ing);
tone rules for low consonants

bòttîi hòk   บทที่ ๖   *Lesson 6*
kamsàp คำศัพท์ *Vocabulary*

gamlang กำลัง	*to be ...ing*
gamlang jà กำลังจะ	*to be going to*
mâi kɔ̂i ... ไม่ค่อย	*not so ...*
mâi ... ləəi ไม่ .... เลย	*not ... at all*
yang-ngai/yàang-rai ยังไง/อย่างไร	*how*
yàak อยาก	*to want to do something¹*
ao เอา	*to want something¹*
kəəi เคย	*ever, used to*
bpà-gà-dtì ปกติ	*normally*
bprà-jam ประจำ	*usually*
bɔ̀i-bɔ̀i/bɔ̀i บ่อยๆ/บ่อย	*often*
yang ยัง	*yet, still*
lέεo แล้ว	*already*
dii ดี	*good*
fang ฟัง	*to listen*
kui คุย	*to chat, talk*
póp/jəə พบ/เจอ	*to meet, find*
nâng นั่ง	*to sit*
yʉʉn ยืน	*to stand*
dəən เดิน	*to walk*
wîng วิ่ง	*to run*
sʉ́ʉ ซื้อ	*to buy*
kǎai ขาย	*to sell*
rɔ́ɔng ร้อง	*to sing, cry out*
dtên เต้น	*to dance*
ram รำ	*to dance (traditional)*

lên เล่น	to play
bpai-hǎa ไปหา	to go to see someone
maa-hǎa มาหา	to come to see someone
kàp ขับ	to drive
kìi ขี่	to ride
dtòk ตก	to fall
ngaan งาน	work
tú-rá ธุระ	errand
pleeng เพลง	song
dooi โดย	by
rót รถ	vehicle, car
rótfai รถไฟ	train
rótfai-dtâai-din รถไฟใต้ดิน	subway
rótbát/rótmee รถบัส/รถเมล์	bus
téksìi แท็กซี่	taxi
sɔ̌ɔng-tɛ̌ɛɔ สองแถว	minibus
sǎam-lɔ́ɔ สามล้อ	tricycle
dtúk-dtúk ตุ๊กๆ	tricycle taxi
mɔɔ-təə-sai มอเตอร์ไซ	motorcycle
jàkgrà-yaan จักรยาน	bicycle
krûangbin เครื่องบิน	airplane
rɯa เรือ	boat, ship
fǒn ฝน	rain
hì-má หิมะ	snow
dtônmáai ต้นไม้	tree
puu-kǎo ภูเขา	mountain
tá-lee ทะเล	sea
mɛ̂ɛ-náam แม่น้ำ	river
din ดิน	soil
lom ลม	wind

fai ไฟ   *fire*

dítsà-gôo ดิสโก้   *disco*

kaa-raa-oo-gè คาราโอเกะ   *karaoke*

kɔ̌ɔ-sǎai gàp ขอสายกับ   *"May I speak with ...?"*

---

1. ' yàak'(อยาก) *and* ' ao' (เอา) *both mean 'to want' but* ' yàak' *is followed by a verb and* ' ao' *is followed by a noun.*

e.g. pǒm yàak taan kà-nǒm. = *I want to eat dessert.*

pǒm ao kà-nǒm. = *I want dessert.*

Sometimes ' ao' *is followed by a verb. In that case it means something other than 'to want'.*

e.g. ' ao bpai' (เอาไป) *means 'to take something ' and not 'to want to go'. ('To want to go' is* 'yàak bpai' (อยากไป).*)*

' ao' (เอา) *also means "to take".*

e.g. ao an níi. = *I take this one.*

Another form of ' ao' (เอา) *is* ' yàak dâai ' (อยากได้) *and the polite form of both words is* ' dtɔ̂ng-gaan' (ต้องการ).

You can say either one of the following when you want to say "I want dessert":

pǒm ao kà-nǒm. (ผมเอาขนม)

pǒm yàak dâai kà-nǒm. (ผมอยากได้ขนม)

pǒm dtɔ̂ng-gaan kà-nǒm. (ผมต้องการขนม)

Conversation

Bancha: hanlŏo. kɔ̌ɔ sǎai gàp kun juu-ĺii kráp.

บัญชา: ฮัลโหล   ขอ สาย กับ คุณ จูลี่ ครับ

Hello! May I speak with Julie?

Julie: gamlang pûut kâ.

จูลี่:   กำลัง   พูด   ค่ะ

Speaking.

Bancha: kun juu-ĺii gamlang tam à-rai kráp.

บัญชา: คุณ จูลี่   กำลัง   ทำ   อะไร ครับ

What are you doing Julie?

Julie: gamlang jà taankâao kâ. kun taankâao ru̇ yang ká.

จูลี่:   กำลัง   จะ ทานข้าว ค่ะ คุณ ทานข้าว รึ ยัง   คะ

I'm going to eat. Have you eaten?

Bancha: taan lέεo kráp.

บัญชา: ทาน แล้ว ครับ

Yes, I have.

wanníi kun yàak bpai kaa-raa-oo-gè mái kráp.

วันนี้   คุณ อยาก ไป   คาราโอเกะ   ไหม ครับ

Do you want to go to karaoke today?

Julie: yàak kâ. chán yang mâi kəəi bpai.

อยาก ค่ะ   ฉัน   ยัง   ไม่ เคย ไป

Yes. I've never been.

bprà-yòok   ประโยค   *Sentences*

1. A: kun gamlang   tam à-rai.
        คุณ กำลัง   ทำ อะไร
        What are you doing?

    B: rao gamlang taan kâao.
        เรา   กำลัง   ทาน ข้าว
        We are eating.

    A: kun gamlang jà tam à-rai.
        คุณ   กำลัง   จะ ทำ อะไร
        What are you going to do?

    B: rao gamlang jà duu tii-wii.
        เรา   กำลัง   จะ ดู ทีวี
        We are going to watch T.V.

2. A: kun taankâao rʉ́ yang.
        คุณ ทานข้าว รึ ยัง
        Have you eaten?

    B: taan lɛ́ɛo.
        ทาน แล้ว
        Yes, I have.

    C: yang mâi taan.
        ยัง ไม่ ทาน
        No, I haven't.

    A: kun duu tii-wii rʉ́ yang.
        คุณ ดู ทีวี รึ ยัง
        Have you watched T.V.?

    B: duu lɛ́ɛo.
        ดู แล้ว
        Yes, I have.

C: yang mâi duu.
    ยัง ไม่ ดู
    No, I haven't.

3. A: kun yàak (jà) tam à-rai.
    คุณ อยาก (จะ) ทำ อะไร
    What do you want to do?

 B: pǒm yàak (jà) taankâao.
    ผม อยาก (จะ) ทานข้าว
    I want to eat.

 C: pǒm yàak (jà) duu tii-wii.
    ผม อยาก (จะ) ดู ทีวี
    I want to watch T.V.

4. A: kun kəəi bpai mɨang tai mái.
    คุณ เคย ไป เมือง ไทย ไหม
    Have you ever been to Thailand?

 B: kəəi.
    เคย
    Yes, I have.

 C: mâi kəəi.
    ไม่ เคย
    No, I haven't.

 A: kun kəəi nâng dtúk-dtúk mái.
    คุณ เคย นั่ง ตุ๊กๆ ไหม
    Have you ever ridden a tricycle taxi?

 B: kəəi lɛ́ɛo.
    เคย แล้ว
    Yes, I already have.

 C: yang mâi kəəi.
    ยัง ไม่ เคย
    No, I haven't.

5. A: an nii mâi kɔ̂i dii.
   อัน นี้ ไม่ ค่อย ดี
   This one is not very good.

   B: pǒm mâi kɔ̂i chɔ̂ɔp aa-hǎan fà-ràng.
   ผม ไม่ ค่อย ชอบ อาหาร ฝรั่ง
   I don't like foreign food very much.

   C: kun sǒmchai mâi kɔ̂i mii ngən.
   คุณ สมชัย ไม่ ค่อย มี เงิน
   Mr. Somchai does not have very much money.

6. A: an nii mâi dii ləəi.
   อัน นี้ ไม่ ดี เลย
   This one is not good at all.

   B: pǒm mâi chɔ̂ɔp aa-hǎan fà-ràng ləəi.
   ผม ไม่ ชอบ อาหาร ฝรั่ง เลย
   I don't like western food at all.

   C: kun sǒmchai mâi mii ngən ləəi.
   คุณ สมชัย ไม่ มี เงิน เลย
   Mr. Somchai does not have any money at all.

7. A: kun sǒmchai bpai taan aa-hǎan tai bprà-jam.
   คุณ สมชัย ไป ทาน อาหาร ไทย ประจำ
   Mr. Somchai goes to eat Thai food regularly.

   B: kun sǒmchai bpai taan aa-hǎan tai bɔ̀i-bɔ̀i.
   คุณ สมชัย ไป ทาน อาหาร ไทย บ่อยๆ
   Mr. Somchai goes to eat Thai food often.

   C: kun sǒmchai bpai taan aa-hǎan tai túk wan-pút.
   คุณ สมชัย ไป ทาน อาหาร ไทย ทุก วันพุธ
   Mr. Somchai goes to eat Thai food every Wednesday.

8. A: bpà-gà-dtì kun bpai tam-ngaan yang-ngai
   ปกติ คุณ ไป ทำงาน ยังไง
   How do you normally go to work?

B: kàp rót bpai.

ขับ รถ ไป

I drive.

C: nâng téksîi bpai.

นั่ง แท็กซี่ ไป

I take a taxi.

D: kìi mɔɔ-təə-sai bpai.

ขี่ มอเตอร์ไซ ไป

I ride a motorcycle.

E: dəən bpai.

เดิน ไป

I walk.

9. A: bpai nǎi maa.

ไป ไหน มา

Where have you been?

B: bpai ginkâao maa.

ไป กินข้าว มา

I went to eat.

A: súu à-rai maa.

ซื้อ อะไร มา

What did you buy?

B: súu kà-nǒm maa.

ซื้อ ขนม มา

I bought snacks.

maa (มา) *at the end of these sentences literally means to have done something and come back, which implies the past tense.*

10. A: pǒm yàak bpai-hǎa kun.

ผม อยาก ไปหา คุณ

I want to go to see you.

B: mûa-waanníi káo maa-hăa dì-chán.

เมื่อวานนี้   เขา มาหา   ดิฉัน

Yesterday he came to see me.

C: káo too-rá-sàp maa-hăa kun.

เขา โทรศัพท์   มาหา   คุณ

He gave you a call.

D: pŏm dəən bpai-hăa káo.

ผม เดิน ไปหา เขา

I walk to (meet) him.

11. fŏn gamlang dtòk.

ฝน   กำลัง   ตก

It's raining.

12. pŏm bpai tam-ngaan dooi rótyon.

ผม ไป   ทำงาน   โดย รถยนต์

I go to work by car.

13. rao chɔ̂ɔp kui gàp kon tai.

เรา ชอบ คุย กับ คน ไทย

We like to talk to Thai people.

14. tîi muang tai mâi mii hì-má.

ที่ เมือง ไทย ไม่ มี หิมะ

There is no snow in Thailand.

15. tîi puu-kăo mâi kɔ̂i mii dtônmáai.

ที่ ภูเขา ไม่ ค่อย มี   ต้นไม้

There are not so many trees in the mountains.

16. tîi bâan mâi mii kon ləəi.

ที่ บ้าน ไม่ มี คน เลย

There isn't anybody at home at all.

17. wanníi mii tú-rá mâak, bpai-hăa kun mâi dâai.

วันนี้   มี   ธุระ มาก   ไปหา คุณ ไม่ ได้

Today, I have a lot of errands. I can't go to see you.

18. pǒm taankâao lέεo.
     ผม   ทานข้าว   แล้ว
     I already ate.

19. pǒm yang mâi taankâao.
     ผม   ยัง   ไม่   ทานข้าว
     I haven't eaten yet.

20. rao nâng fang pleeng.
     เรา   นั่ง   ฟัง   เพลง
     We listened to music.

     No. 20 literally means "We sat and listened to the music."

21. káo yuun kui gàp kun.
     เขา   ยืน   คุย   กับ   คุณ
     He talked to you.

     No. 21 literally means "He stood and talked to you."

22. pǒm chɔ̂ɔp nâng àan nǎngsǔu tîi bâan.
     ผม   ชอบ   นั่ง   อ่าน   หนังสือ   ที่   บ้าน
     I like to read at home.

     1. No. 22 literally means "I like to sit and read at home".

     2. àan nǎngsǔu means to read a book and it also means to read anything in general.

23. prûng-níi yàak bpai-tîao gàp fεεn.
     พรุ่งนี้   อยาก   ไปเที่ยว   กับ   แฟน
     Tomorrow I want to go out with my girlfriend.

24. káo yang mâi yàak rian paa-sǎa tai dtɔɔnníi.
     เขา   ยัง   ไม่   อยาก   เรียน   ภาษา   ไทย   ตอนนี้
     He doesn't want to study Thai at the moment.

25. .wanníi mâi yàak tam à-rai.
     วันนี้   ไม่   อยาก   ทำ   อะไร
     Today I don't want to do anything.

Test 6

Match the English verbs with the Thai verbs.

_____	1. *to talk*	a. fang	ฟัง
_____	2. *to listen*	b. wîng	วิ่ง
_____	3. *to take a trip*	c. dtòk	ตก
_____	4. *to play*	d. róɔng	ร้อง
_____	5. *to wake up*	e. dəən	เดิน
_____	6. *to drive*	f. pûut	พูด
_____	7. *to sit*	g. yɯɯn	ยืน
_____	8. *to run*	h. bpai-tîao	ไปเที่ยว
_____	9. *to walk*	i. lên	เล่น
_____	10. *to buy*	j. àan	อ่าน
_____	11. *to sell*	k. sɯ́ɯ	ซื้อ
_____	12. *to sing*	l. dtɯ̀ɯn	ตื่น
_____	13. *to fall*	m. yàak	อยาก
_____	14. *to want to*	n. nâng	นั่ง
_____	15. *to stand*	o. kui	คุย
		p. kàp	ขับ
		q. kăai	ขาย

Translate the following into English.

1. dtɔɔnníi dì-chán gamlang jà bpai sà-năambin
    ตอนนี้   ดิฉัน   กำลัง   จะ ไป   สนามบิน

    _____

2. bpà-gà-dtì kun sŏmchai nâng rótfai bpai tam-ngaan.
    ปกติ   คุณ สมชัย   นั่ง รถไฟ ไป   ทำงาน

    _____

3. rao yàak mii ráan aa-hăan tai tîi à-mee-rí-gaa
    เรา อยาก มี ร้าน อาหาร ไทย ที่   อเมริกา

    _____

4. kăo yùu mɨang tai dtâng-dtὲε dɨan mí-tù-naa
    เขา อยู่ เมือง ไทย ตั้งแต่   เดือน มิถุนา

    _____

5. pŏm mâi kɔ̂i chɔ̂ɔp fang pleeng.
    ผม ไม่ ค่อย ชอบ ฟัง เพลง

    _____

Practice Writing the Low Consonants

Except for ญ /y/, all the low consonants are written with one stroke. Start near the **❶**. We have already practiced five letters in the final consonants section in Lesson 3.

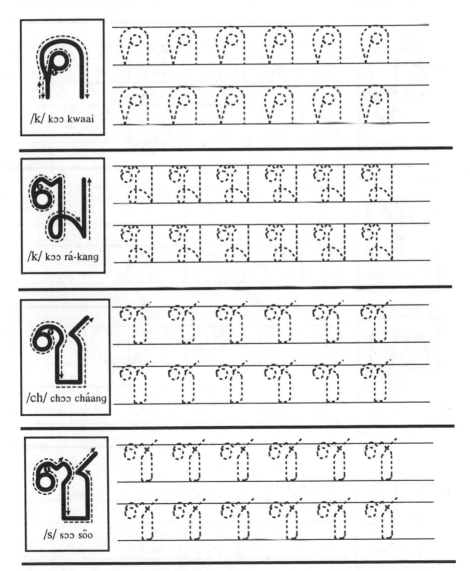

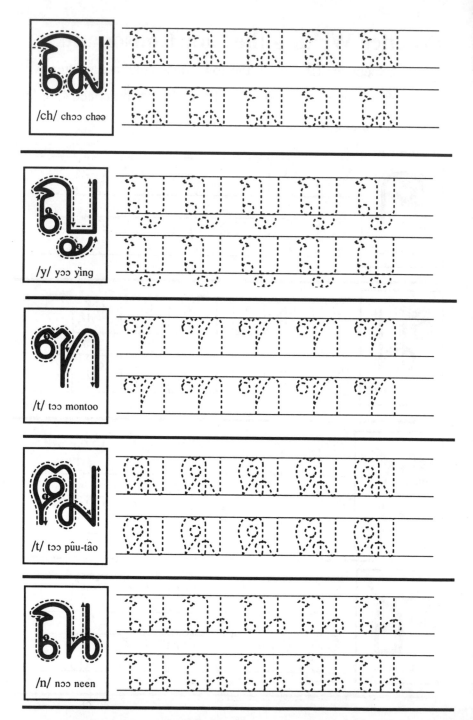

/ch/ chɔɔ chəə

/y/ yɔɔ yǐng

/t/ tɔɔ montoo

/t/ tɔɔ pûu-tâo

/n/ nɔɔ neen

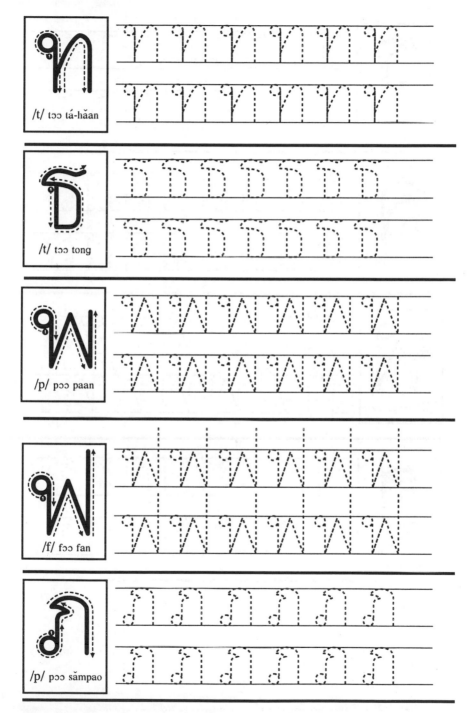

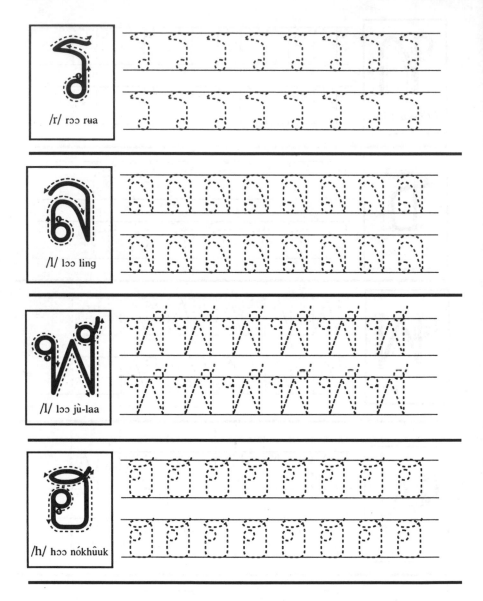

/r/ rɔɔ rɯa

/l/ lɔɔ liŋ

/l/ lɔɔ jùu-laa

/h/ hɔɔ nókhûuk

Tone Rules for Low Consonants

In the absence of a tone mark, the tone rules for low consonants are as follows:

Low Consonant with <u>Live Syllable = Mid Tone</u>

Low Consonant with Short Vowel and <u>Dead Syllable = High Tone</u>

Low Consonant with Long Vowel and <u>Dead Syllable = Falling Tone</u>

Notice that there are two kinds of dead syllables with the low consonants. The first kind has a <u>short vowel</u> either in final position or followed by a stop final. The second kind has a <u>long vowel</u> followed by a stop final.

Examples:

Low Consonant + Long Vowel = Live syllable

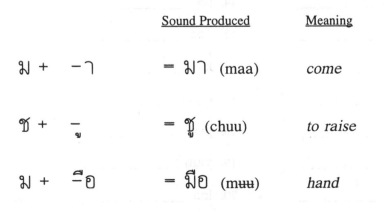

	<u>Sound Produced</u>	<u>Meaning</u>
ม + ‑า	= มา (maa)	*come*
ช + ◌ู	= ชู (chuu)	*to raise*
ม + ื◌อ	= มือ (muu)	*hand*

Exercise: <u>Read the Following Words and Practice Writing Them</u> <u>in Thai.</u>

1. เมีย   *wife*   2. วัว   *ox*

3. พอ   *enough*   4. ไฟ   *fire*

5. ลา   *donkey*   6. ที   *time*

7. เรือ   *ship*   8. นาย   *Mr.*

9. เมา   *drunk*   10. งู   *snake*

11. ใน   *in*   12. ยา   *medicine*

13. เรา   *we*   14. เนย   *butter*

Writing Exercise 6

Transcribe the following into Thai script. Use ค, ช, ท, น, พ, ย, and ล for the /k/, /ch/, /t/ /n/, /p/, /y/ and /l/ sounds respectivly.

1. paa _____   11. tii _____

2. choo _____   12. yɔɔ _____

3. ram _____   13. fuu _____

4. moo _____   14. tee _____

5. sia _____   15. kɔɔ _____

6. lia _____   16. kɰɰ _____

7. chəəi _____   17. ngaa _____

8. tua _____   18. pɛɛ _____

9. rɰa _____   19. yam _____

10. fao _____   20. laa _____

Lesson 7

'dâi-yin'ˎ(to hear);   'jam' (to remember);
'nɔɔn-làp'(to fall asleep);   'mɔɔng' (to look);
tone rules for low consonants (cont.)

bòttîi jèt   บทที่ ๗   *Lesson 7*

kamsàp คำศัพท์ *Vocabulary*

krai ใคร	*who*
kɔ̌ɔng ของ	*of*
kɔ̌ɔng krai ของใคร	*whose*
bpen/dâai เป็น/ได้	*can*
mâi bpen/mâi dâai ไม่เป็น/ไม่ได้	*cannot*
mâi dâai ไม่ได้	*did not*
wâai-náam/wâai ว่ายน้ำ	*to swim*
jam จำ	*to memorize*
jam dâai จำได้	*to remember*
jam mâi dâai จำไม่ได้	*can't remember*
jam dâai mái จำได้ไหม	*Do you remember?*
dâi-yin ได้ยิน	*to hear, can hear*
mâi dâi-yin ไม่ได้ยิน	*can't hear*
dâi-yin mái ได้ยินไหม	*Can you hear?*
mɔɔng/mɔɔngduu มอง/มองดู	*to look*
(mɔɔng) hěn (มอง) เห็น	*to see, can see*
(mɔɔng) mâi hěn (มอง) ไม่เห็น	*can't see*
(mɔɔng) hěn mái (มอง) เห็นไหม	*Can you see?*
rúu/sâap/rúu-jàk รู้/ทราบ/รู้จัก	*to know*[1]
nɔɔn làp นอนหลับ	*to fall asleep*
nɔɔn mâi làp นอนไม่หลับ	*can't fall asleep*
sèt เสร็จ	*to finish*
ngûang/ngûang-nɔɔn ง่วง/ง่วงนอน	*sleepy*
dang/sǐang dang ดัง/เสียงดัง	*loud*

nùak-hǔu หนวกหู	bothered by loud noise
nùai เหนื่อย	tired
tan ทัน	on time, to keep up with
ɔ̀ɔk ออก	out
kít คิด	to think
kíttǔng คิดถึง	to think about, miss
kít wâa คิดว่า	to think that ...
tùuk ถูก	correct
pìt ผิด	incorrect
jing/jing-jing จริง/จริงๆ	true, really
à-rɔ̀i อร่อย	delicious
wǎan หวาน	sweet
kem เค็ม	salty
jùut จืด	tasteless
bprîao เปรี้ยว	sour
pèt เผ็ด	spicy, hot

1. sâap -"to know" is a polite form of rúu . Both sâap and
    rúu are used without an object. rúu-jàk can be used
    with or without an object.
    e.g. pǒm mâi rúu. or pǒm mâi sâap. = I don't know
          pǒm mâi rúu-jàk káo. = I don't know him.
          We don't say, " pǒm mâi rúu káo."

Conversation

Jane: bâan kun wí-nai yùu tîi-nǎi ká.

เจน: บ้าน คุณ วินัย อยู่ ที่ไหน คะ

Where is your house, Winai?

Winai: yùu tîi à-yúttá-yaa. kun rúu-jàk mái kráp.

วินัย: อยู่ ที่ อยุธยา คุณ รู้จัก ไหม ครับ

In Ayutthaya. Do you know where that is?

Jane: rúu-jàk kâ.

เจน: รู้จัก ค่ะ

Yes, I do.

Winai: kun maa mɯang tai mɯ̂a-rài kráp.

วินัย: คุณ มา เมือง ไทย เมื่อไหร่ ครับ

When did you come to Thailand?

Jane: bprà-maan sǎam bpii lɛ́ɛo kâ.

เจน: ประมาณ สาม ปี แล้ว ค่ะ

About three years ago.

Winai: kun chɔ̂ɔp aa-hǎan tai mái kráp.

วินัย: คุณ ชอบ อาหาร ไทย ไหม ครับ

Do you like Thai food?

Jane: chɔ̂ɔp kâ. aa-hǎan tai à-rɔ̀i mâak. dì-chán chɔ̂ɔp pèt.

เจน: ชอบ ค่ะ อาหาร ไทย อร่อย มาก ดิฉัน ชอบ เผ็ด

Yes. Thai food is very good. I like spicy food.

Winai: kun àan paa-sǎa tai ɔ̀ɔk mái kráp.

วินัย: คุณ อ่าน ภาษา ไทย ออก ไหม ครับ

Can you read Thai?

Jane: àan ɔ̀ɔk nítnɔ̀i. dtɛ̀ɛ kǐan mâi dâai.

เจน: อ่าน ออก นิดหน่อย แต่ เขียน ไม่ ได้

I can read a little, but I can't write.

Winai: fang tan mái kráp.

วินัย: ฟัง   ทัน ไหม ครับ

Can you understand (spoken Thai)?

(Literally: Can you catch up with listening?)

Jane: tâa pûut cháa-cháa, fang tan kâ.

เจน: ถ้า พูด   ช้าๆ   ฟัง   ทัน ค่ะ

If (you) speak slowly, I can understand.

tâa pûut reo-reo, fang mâi kɔ̂i tan.

ถ้า พูด เร็วๆ   ฟัง ไม่ ค่อย ทัน

If (you) speak fast, I don't understand very well.

bprà-yòok   ประโยค   *Sentences*

1. A: nîi krai.
       นี่ ใคร
       Who is this?

    B: nîi kun somchai.
       นี่ คุณ สมชัย
       This is Mr. Somchai.

2. A: nîi kɔ̌ɔng krai.
       นี่ ของ ใคร
       Whose is this?

    B: nîi kɔ̌ɔng pǒm.
       นี่ ของ ผม
       This is mine.

    A: nîi bâan (kɔ̌ɔng)* krai.
       นี่ บ้าน (ของ)   ใคร
       Whose house is this?

    B: nîi bâan (kɔ̌ɔng) pǒm.
       นี่ บ้าน (ของ) ผม
       This is my house.

    * kɔ̌ɔng *can be omitted when used with noun.*

3. A: kun wâai-náam bpen mái.
       คุณ   ว่ายน้ำ   เป็น ไหม
       Can you swim?

    B: wâai bpen.
       ว่าย เป็น
       Yes, I can.

    C: wâai mâi bpen.
       ว่าย ไม่ เป็น
       No, I can't.

4. A: jam pǒm dâai mái.
       จำ   ผม   ได้ ไหม
       Do you remember me?

    B: jam dâai.*
       จำ   ได้
       Yes, I do.

    C: jam mâi dâai.
       จำ ไม่ ได้
       No, I don't.

5. A: dâi-yin* mái.
       ได้ยิน ไหม
       Can you hear?

    B: dâi-yin.*
       ได้ยิน
       Yes, I can.

    C: mâi dâi-yin.*
       ไม่ ได้ยิน
       No, I can't.

6. A: mɔɔng-hěn káo mái.
       มองเห็น   เขา ไหม
       Can you see him?

*ไ- *in* jam dâai (จำได้) *sounds longer than* ไ- *in* dâi-yin (ได้ยิน).

B: mɔɔng-hĕn.
   มองเห็น
   Yes, I can.

C: mɔɔng mâi hĕn.
   มอง   ไม่   เห็น
   No, I can't.

7. A: rúu-jàk káo mái.
      รู้จัก   เขา ไหม
      Do you know him?

   B: rúu-jàk.
      รู้จัก
      Yes, I do.

   C: mâi rúu-jàk.
      ไม่   รู้จัก
      No, I don't.

8. A: sèt rú yang.
      เสร็จ รี ยัง
      Are you ready?/Have you finished?

   B: sèt lέεo.
      เสร็จ แล้ว
      Yes, I am./Yes, I have.

   C: yang mâi sèt.
      ยัง   ไม่ เสร็จ
      No, I'm not./No, I haven't.

9.   mûa-kɯɯn-níi nɔɔn mâi kɔ̂i làp.
      เมื่อคืนนี้   นอน ไม่ ค่อย หลับ
      I didn't sleep very well last night.

10.   mûa-kɯɯn-níi nɔɔn làp sà-baai.
      เมื่อคืนนี้   นอน หลับ สบาย
      I slept very well last night.

11. A: ngûang-nɔɔn jing-jing.

ง่วงนอน   จริงๆ

I'm really sleepy.

   B: nùai jing-jing.

เหนื่อย จริงๆ

I'm really tired.

   C: nùak-hǔu jing-jing.

หนวกหู   จริงๆ

It's really noisy.

   D: dii jing-jing.

ดี   จริงๆ

It's really good.

12.   sǐang dang mâak.

เสียง ดัง มาก

The noise is very loud.

13.   káo fang paa-sǎa tai mâi tan.

เขา ฟัง ภาษา ไทย ไม่ ทัน

He can't understand spoken Thai.

(Literally: He can't keep up with listening to the Thai language.)

14.   àan nǎngsǔu-pim paa-sǎa tai mâi ɔ̀ɔk.*

อ่าน หนังสือพิมพ์ ภาษา ไทย ไม่ ออก

I can't read Thai newspapers.

15.   gin pèt mâi dâai.

กิน เผ็ด ไม่ ได้

I can't eat hot food.

16.   mâi dâai gin pèt.

ไม่ ได้ กิน เผ็ด

I didn't eat hot food.

* ɔ̀ɔk *is often used with the verbs,* pûut, àan, kǐan.

   e.g. fang mâi ɔ̀ɔk. *or* fang mâi dâai. = *I don't/can't understand.*

17. bpai mʉang tai mâi dâai.
     ไป เมือง ไทย ไม่ ได้
     I can't go to Thailand.

18. mâi dâai bpai mʉang tai.
     ไม่ ได้ ไป เมือง ไทย
     I didn't go to Thailand.
     Be careful when using "mâi dâai". When it comes before verbs,
     it means "did not"; but when it comes after verbs, it means "cannot".

19. pǒm kíttʉ̌ng kun mâak.
     ผม คิดถึง คุณ มาก
     I miss you very much.

20. rao gamlang mɔɔng duu tá-lee.
     เรา กำลัง มอง ดู ทะเล
     We are looking at the sea.

21. pǒm pûut paa-sǎa tai mâi kɔ̂i tùuk.
     ผม พูด ภาษา ไทย ไม่ ค่อย ถูก
     I don't speak Thai very correctly.

22. káo àan paa-sǎa ang-grìt mâi pìt ləəi.
     เขา อ่าน ภาษา อังกฤษ ไม่ ผิด เลย
     He reads English without making mistakes.
     (Literally: He reads English not incorrectly at all.)

23. A: pǒm kít wâa à-rɔ̀i.
       ผม คิด ว่า อร่อย
       I think it's delicious.

    B: pǒm kít wâa aa-hǎan tai à-rɔ̀i.
       ผม คิด ว่า อาหาร ไทย อร่อย
       I think Thai food is delicious.

    C: pǒm kít wâa aa-hǎan tai à-rɔ̀i jing-jing.
       ผม คิด ว่า อาหาร ไทย อร่อย จริงๆ
       I think Thai food is really delicious.

    A: pǒm kít wâa pèt.
       ผม คิด ว่า เผ็ด
       I think it's spicy.

B: pǒm kít wâa aa-hǎan tai pèt.

ผม คิด ว่า อาหาร ไทย เผ็ด

I think Thai food is spicy.

C: pǒm kít wâa aa-hǎan tai pèt jing-jing.

ผม คิด ว่า อาหาร ไทย เผ็ด จริงๆ

I think Thai food is really spicy.

24. A: kun kít wâa jà bpai mɯang tai mɯ̂a-rài.

คุณ คิด ว่า จะไป เมือง ไทย เมื่อไหร่

When do you think you will go to Thailand?

B: kít wâa jà bpai dɯan-nâa.

คิด ว่า จะ ไป เดือนหน้า

I think I will go next month.

25. A: káo chɯ̂ɯ à-rai.

เขา ชื่อ อะไร

What's his name?

B: mâi rúu. kít mâi ɔ̀ɔk.

ไม่ รู้ คิด ไม่ ออก

I don't know. I can't think of it.

(*Literally: I can't think it out.*)

Test 7

Match the English words with the Thai words.

_____ 1. *tired*   a. pìt ผิด

_____ 2. *sleepy*   b. jing-jing จริงๆ

_____ 3. *to think about* c. bprîao เปรี้ยว

_____ 4. *to hear*   d. kíttǔng คิดถึง

_____ 5. *sweet*   e. dang ดัง

_____ 6. *salty*   f. à-rɔ̀i อร่อย

_____ 7. *incorrect*   g. pèt เผ็ด

_____ 8. *to remember*   h. ngûang-nɔɔn ง่วงนอน

_____ 9. *to finish*   i. tùuk ถูก

_____ 10. *delicious*   j. wǎan หวาน

_____ 11. *sour*   k. sèt เสร็จ

_____ 12. *who*   l. kít คิด

_____ 13. *loud*   m. nùai เหนื่อย

_____ 14. *really*   n. kem เค็ม

_____ 15. *correct*   o. jam dâai จำได้

                           p. dâi-yin ได้ยิน

                           q. krai ใคร

Translate the following into English.

1. sà-mùt kɔ̌ɔng krai yùu bon dtó.
   สมุด   ของ   ใคร อยู่ บน โต๊ะ

_____

2. pǒm wâai-náam mâi dâai.
   ผม   ว่ายน้ำ   ไม่ ได้

_____

3. pǒm mâi dâai wâai-náam.
   ผม ไม่ ได้   ว่ายน้ำ

_____

4. káo kíttǔng mɯang tai mâak jing-jing.
   เขา คิดถึง   เมือง ไทย มาก   จริงๆ

_____

5. dì-chán kít wâa aa-hǎan fà-ràng mâi kɔ̂i à-rɔ̀i.
   ดิฉัน คิด ว่า อาหาร   ฝรั่ง   ไม่ ค่อย อร่อย

_____

Tone Rules for Low Consonants (cont.)

In the absence of a tone mark, the tone rules for low consonants are as follows:

Low Consonant with <u>Live Syllable = Mid Tone</u>

Low Consonant with Long Vowel and <u>Dead Syllable = Falling Tone</u>

Low Consonant with Short Vowel and <u>Dead Syllable = High Tone</u>

Examples:

Low Consonant + Short Vowel = Dead syllable

		<u>Sound Produced</u>	<u>Meaning</u>
ค +	-ะ	= คะ (ká)	*polite particle for women*
ล +	เ-ะ	= เละ (lé)	*mushy*

Exercise: <u>Read the Following Words and Practice Writing Them in Thai.</u>

1. เคาะ	*to knock*	2. รึ	*or*
3. เงาะ	*rambutan*	4. เลอะ	*dirty, splattered*
5. เยอะ	*a lot*	6. ละ	*per*
7. แวะ	*to stop over*	8. ธุระ	*errand*
9. แพะ	*goat*	10. และ	*and*

Low Consonant + Any Vowel + Sonorant Final

= Live syllable

			Sound Produced	Meaning
ล +	◌ี	+ ง	= ลิง (ling)	*monkey*
ม +	◌ั	+ น	= มัน (man)	*it*
ย +	-า	+ ย	= ยาย (yaai)	*grandmother*

Low Consonant + Long Vowel + Stop Final

= Dead syllable (Falling Tone)

		Sound Produced	Meaning
ค + -า + บ		= คาบ (kâap)	*to hold something between the teeth*
ล + ◌ู + ก		= ลูก (lûuk)	*child*
ม + ◌ี + ด		= มีด (mîit)	*knife*

Low Consonant + Short Vowel + Stop Final

= Dead syllable (High Tone)

		Sound Produced	Meaning
ค + ◌ั + บ		= คับ (káp)	*tight*
ล + ◌ุ + ก		= ลุก (lúk)	*to rise*
ม + ◌ิ + ด		= มิด (mít)	*entirely*

Exercise: <u>Read the Following Words and Practice Writing Them</u>
<u>in Thai. Also Identify the Tones.</u>

1. ซุง   *log*   2. มืด   *dark*

3. เล็ก   *small*   4. มาก   *many*

5. ทับ   *to put on top*   6. นัด   *appointment*

7. ราด   *to pour over*   8. ฟาง   *hay*

9. วัน   *day*   10. ลบ   *to subtract*

11. รับ   *to receive*   12. ยุง   *mosquito*

13. โลก   *earth*   14. ชุด   *set*

15. นวด   *to massage*   16. นาย   *Mr.*

17. พัง   *to collapse*   18. ทาก   *snail*

19. รัก   *to love*   20. เทียม   *fake*

Tone Marks With Low Consonants

With low consonant syllables, there are three possible tones and two tone marks which may be used.

Tone Mark	Tone Name	Tone	Examples
่	sĭang too	*falling*	ค่า (kâa)
้	sĭang drii	*high*	ค้า (káa)

The third possible tone, mid tone, occurs with live syllables and no tone marks. (Review "Tone Rules for Low Consonants" on page 160.)

Exercise: <u>Read the Following Words and Practice Writing Them in Thai. Also Identify the Tones.</u>

1. ม่วง   *purple*
2. นั้น   *that*
3. ชิ้น   *piece*
4. ซ่อน   *to hide*
5. ฟ้า   *sky*
6. ว่าง   *free*
7. ล้น   *to overflow*
8. ม้า   *horse*
9. นี้   *this*
10. พี่   *older sibling*

Read The Following Aloud

1. คา   ค่า   ค้า

2. ชี   ชี่   ชี้

3. ชู   ชู่   ชู้

4. เท   เท่   เท้

5. ไฟ   ไฟ่   ไฟ้

6. เนา   เน่า   เน้า

7. พอ   พ่อ   พ้อ

8. โม   โม่   โม้

9. แย   แย่   แย้

10. รือ   รื่อ   รื้อ

11. เลย   เล่ย   เล้ย

12. โว   โว่   โว้

Writing Exercise 7

Transcribe the following into Thai script. Use ค, ช, ท, น, พ, ย, and ล for the initial /k/, /ch/, /t/ /n/, /p/, /y/ and /l/ sounds respectively.

1. mûang _____

2. nók _____

3. kâm _____

4. yuung _____

5. fiim _____

6. níu _____

7. mîit _____

8. sɔɔng _____

9. fang _____

10. wɛɛo _____

11. chaam _____

12. rîap _____

13. puum _____

14. ráan _____

15. hâap _____

16. wâang _____

17. yüang _____

18. chêng _____

19. kók _____

20. püa _____

Lesson 8

Body parts; everyday life; special อ; silent ห

bòttîi bpèet   บทที่ ๘   *Lesson 8*
kamsàp   คำศัพท์   *Vocabulary*

dtaa	ตา	*eye*
hǔu	หู	*ear*
jà-mùuk	จมูก	*nose*
bpàak	ปาก	*mouth*
fan	ฟัน	*tooth*
líin	ลิ้น	*tongue*
nùat	หนวด	*mustache*
krao	เครา	*beard*
lák-yím	ลักยิ้ม	*dimple*
kíu	คิ้ว	*eyebrow*
pǒm	ผม	*hair (on the head only)[1]*
kǒn	ขน	*hair*
kǒn-dtaa	ขนตา	*eyelash*
hǔa	หัว	*head*
nâa	หน้า	*face*
nâa-pàak	หน้าผาก	*forehead*
lǎng	หลัง	*back*
kɔɔ	คอ	*neck*
tɔ́ɔng	ท้อง	*stomach*
sà-duu	สะดือ	*navel*
hǔa-jai	หัวใจ	*heart*
nom	นม	*breast*
òk	อก	*chest*
muu	มือ	*hand*
níu/níu-muu	นิ้ว/นิ้วมือ	*finger*
lép	เล็บ	*nail*
kɛ̌ɛn	แขน	*arm*

kǎa ขา	leg
hǔa-kào หัวเข่า	knee
táao เท้า	foot
níu-táao นิ้วเท้า	toe
fǎi ไฝ	mole
sǐu สิว	pimple
náam-dtaa น้ำตา	tear
sà-mɔ̌ɔng สมอง	brain
dtàp ตับ	liver
dtai ไต	kidney
sâi ไส้	intestine
pung พุง	fat stomach, paunch
grà-dùuk กระดูก	bone
dtua ตัว	body
kɔ̌ɔng ของ	thing
sɯ́ɯ-kɔ̌ɔng ซื้อของ	to shop, to buy things
bpai chɔ́p-bpîng ไปชอปปิ้ง	to go shopping
sài ใส่	to wear, put on
tɔ̀ɔt ถอด	to take off
dtɛ̀ng-dtua แต่งตัว	to get dressed
bpùat ปวด	to ache[2]
jèp เจ็บ	to hurt[2]
bpen wàt เป็นหวัด	to catch a cold
dtàt ตัด	to cut
goon โกน	to shave
láang ล้าง	to wash
sà-pǒm สระผม	to wash hair
àap-náam อาบน้ำ	to take a bath/ shower
sákpâa ซักผ้า	to do the laundry
bprɛɛng fan แปรงฟัน	to brush one's teeth

bprεεng-sĭi-fan แปรงสีฟัน	*toothbrush*
yaa-sĭi-fan ยาสีฟัน	*toothpaste*
sà-bùu สบู่	*soap*
fép/pŏng-sák-fɔ̂ɔk แฟ้บ/ผงซักฟอก	*detergent*
mùak หมวก	*hat*
sน̂a เสื้อ	*shirt, blouse*
sน̂a-yน̂นt เสื้อยืด	*T-shirt*
sน̂a-nɔ̂ɔk เสื้อนอก	*business suit*
sน̂a-kɛ̌ɛn-yaao เสื้อแขนยาว	*long-sleeved shirt*
sน̂a-kɛ̌ɛn-sân เสื้อแขนสั้น	*short-sleeved shirt*
néktái เน็คไท	*necktie*
kĕmkàt เข็มขัด	*belt*
kĕmglàt เข็มกลัด	*pin, brooch*
rɔɔng-táao รองเท้า	*shoe*
tŭng-táao ถุงเท้า	*sock*
tŭng-mนน ถุงมือ	*glove*
tŭng-nɔ̂ng ถุงน่อง	*panty hose*
grà-bproong กระโปรง	*skirt*
gaang-geeng กางเกง	*trousers*
dtûm-hŭu ตุ้มหู	*earring*
wɛ̌ɛn แหวน	*ring*
gamlai กำไล	*bracelet*

1. pŏm (ผม) - ' hair' and pŏm- 'I' (ผม) *are spelled and pronounced the same. We understand the meaning from the context.*

2. *both* bpùat *and* jèp *mean 'to have pain', but* jèp *refers to surface pain such as from a cut, scrape, rash or other skin injury.* bpùat (ปวด) *refers to an ache beneath the surface of the skin. When saying "I have a headache" or similar phrase, don't say* ' mii bpùat hŭa'. *Just say* 'bpùat hŭa'.

sɔ̂i/sɔ̂i-kɔɔ สร้อย/สร้อยคอ	necklace
boo โบว์	ribbon
kɔ̌ɔng ของ	thing
lá ละ	per
kráng ครั้ง	time
bpen à-rai เป็นอะไร	"What's the matter?"

Conversation

Ron: kun sù-daa sà-baai dii mái kráp.

รอน: คุณ สุดา สบาย ดี ไหม ครับ

    Suda, how are you doing?

Suda: mâi kɔ̂i sà-baai kâ.

สุดา: ไม่ ค่อย สบาย ค่ะ

    Not so well.

Ron: bpen à-rai kráp.

รอน: เป็น อะไร ครับ

    What's the matter?

Suda: wannii bpùat hǔa mâak. kít wâa jà bpen wàt.

สุดา: วันนี้ ปวด หัว มาก คิด ว่า จะ เป็น หวัด

    Today I have a bad headache. I think I will have a cold.

Ron: bpai-hǎa mɔ̌ɔ rɯ́ yang kráp.

รอน: ไปหา หมอ รึ ยัง ครับ

    Have you gone to see a doctor?

Suda: yang mâi dâai bpai kâ. jà bpai prûng-nii.

สุดา: ยัง ไม่ ได้ ไป ค่ะ จะ ไป พรุ่งนี้

    I haven't gone yet. I will go tomorrow.

kun rɔɔn sà-baai dii rɨ́ ká.

คุณ รอน สบาย ดี รึ คะ

How are you doing, Ron?

Ron: sà-baai dii kráp. dtὲὲ aa-tít tîi-lέεo bpùat fan nítnɔ̀i.

รอน: สบาย ดี ครับ แต่ อาทิตย์ ที่แล้ว ปวด ฟัน นิดหน่อย

I'm fine. But last week I had a little bit of a toothache.

Suda: wanníi kun jà tam à-rai ká.

สุดา: วันนี้ คุณ จะ ทำ อะไร คะ

What will you do today?

Ron: jà bpai sɨ́ɨ-kɔ̌ɔng tîi sǐi-lom *.

รอน: จะ ไป ซื้อของ ที่ สีลม

I will go shopping at Silom.

Suda: jà sɨ́ɨ à-rai ká.

สุดา: จะ ซื้อ อะไร คะ

What will you buy?

Ron: yàak sɨ́ɨ sɨ̂a gàp rɔɔng-táao.

รอน: อยาก ซื้อ เสื้อ กับ รองเท้า

I want to buy shirts and shoes.

* sǐi-lom *is an area in downtown Bangkok.*

bprà-yòok ประโยค *Sentences*

1. A: rao gamlang sài sนิa.

    เรา กำลัง ใส่ เสื้อ

    We are wearing (putting on) our shirts.

    B: káo sài sนิa-nɔ̂ɔk sǐi náam-ngən gàp néktái sǐi dɛɛng.

    เขา ใส่ เสื้อนอก สี น้ำเงิน กับ เน็คไท สี แดง

    He is wearing a blue business jacket and a red necktie.

2. A: káo sài sนิa sǐi à-rai.

    เขา ใส่ เสื้อ สี อะไร

    What color shirt is he wearing?

    B: káo sài sนิa sǐi kǎao.

    เขา ใส่ เสื้อ สี ขาว

    He is wearing a white shirt.

3. prûng-níi jà bpai dtàt pǒm.

    พรุ่งนี้ จะ ไป ตัด ผม

    Tomorrow I will go get a haircut.

4. pǒm goon nùat túk cháao.

    ผม โกน หนวด ทุก เช้า

    I shave my mustache every morning.

5. kon tai chɔ̂ɔp àap-náam.

    คนไทย ชอบ อาบน้ำ

    Thai people like to take baths.

6. A: kun ginkâao wan lá gìi kráng.

    คุณ กินข้าว วัน ละ กี่ ครั้ง

    How many times a day do you eat a meal?

    B: pǒm ginkâao wan lá sǎam kráng.

    ผม กินข้าว วัน ละ สาม ครั้ง

    I eat three times a day.

7. A: kun sákpâa aa-tít lá gìi kráng.

คุณ ซักผ้า อาทิตย์ ละ กี่ ครั้ง

How many times a week do you do the laundry?

B: dì-chán sákpâa aa-tít lá sɔ̌ɔng kráng.

ดิฉัน ซักผ้า อาทิตย์ ละ สอง ครั้ง

I do the laundry twice a week.

8. wanníi bpùat fan jing-jing.

วันนี้ ปวด ฟัน จริงๆ

Today I really have a bad toothache.

9. jà bpai láang mɯɯ tîi hɔ̂ng-náam.

จะ ไป ล้าง มือ ที่ ห้องน้ำ

I will go wash my hands in the bathroom.

10. yàak mii nùat.

อยาก มี หนวด

I want to have a mustache.

11. jèp hǔa-kào.

เจ็บ หัวเข่า

My knees hurt.

12. rao mii hâa níu.

เรา มี ห้า นิ้ว

We have five fingers.

13. pǒm jà bpai sɯ́ɯ sà-bùu gàp yaa-sǐi-fan.

ผม จะ ไป ซื้อ สบู่ กับ ยาสีฟัน

I will go to buy soap and toothpaste.

14. káo chɔ̂ɔp sài sɯ̂a-kɛ̌ɛn-yaao.

เขา ชอบ ใส่ เสื้อแขนยาว

He likes to wear long sleeved shirts.

15. káo mii pung nítnɔ̀i.

เขา มี พุง นิดหน่อย

He has a little paunch.

Test 8

Match the English words with the Thai words.

_____ 1. *hand*   a. rɔɔng-táao   รองเท้า

_____ 2. *to wash*   b. hǔu   หู

_____ 3. *face*   c. kǎa   ขา

_____ 4. *to take a bath*   d. mɯɯ   มือ

_____ 5. *head*   e. hǔa   หัว

_____ 6. *to cut*   f. bpùat   ปวด

_____ 7. *leg*   g. grà-bproong   กระโปรง

_____ 8. *shoe*   h. àap-náam   อาบน้ำ

_____ 9. *skirt*   i. nâa   หน้า

_____ 10. *hair*   j. sákpâa   ซักผ้า

_____ 11. *hat*   k. mùak   หมวก

_____ 12. *ear*   l. sà-bùu   สบู่

_____ 13. *soap*   m. láang   ล้าง

_____ 14. *to do the laundry* n. pǒm   ผม

_____ 15. *to have pain*   o. tǔng-táao   ถุงเท้า

                                 p. dtàt   ตัด

                                 q. gaang-geeng   กางเกง

Translate the following into English.

1. A: kun bprɛɛng-fan wan lá gìi kráng.
    คุณ แปรงฟัน   วัน ละ กี่ ครั้ง

    _____

    B: wan lá sɔ̌ɔng kráng.
    วัน ละ สอง   ครั้ง

    _____

2. káo bpùat hǔa mâak.   maa tam-ngaan mâi dâai.
    เขา ปวด หัว มาก   มา ทำงาน ไม่ ได้

    _____

3. dì-chán sà-pǒm túk wan.
    ดิฉัน สระผม ทุก วัน

    _____

4. sǒmchai mii lák-yím.
    สมชัย มี   ลักยิ้ม

    _____

5. kun mâi mii sà-mɔ̌ɔng.
    คุณ ไม่ มี   สมอง

    _____

Special อ

There are four words in the Thai language which use the silent อ to change the word's tone characteristics. Try to memorize them. Notice that in these words the low class consonant ย takes on the tone characteristics of the middle consonant อ.

	Sound Produced	Meaning
อ + ย่า	= อย่า (yàa)	*do not*
อ + ยู่	= อยู่ (yùu)	*to live, to be*
อ + ยาก	= อยาก (yàak)	*to want*
อ + ย่าง	= อย่าง (yàang)	*kind*

Silent ห

A silent ห is called "hɔ̌ɔ-nam". It may appear before the following eight low consonants. In this case, the low consonant takes on all the tone characteristics of the high consonant ห. When a tone mark appears, it is placed over the low consonant, not over the silent ห.

1. ง

2. ญ

3. น

4. ม

5. ย

6. ร

7. ล

8. ว

		Sound Produced		Meaning
ห + งอก	=	หงอก	(ngɔ̀ɔk)	*gray hair*
ห + ญ้า	=	หญ้า	(yâa)	*grass*
ห + นี้	=	หนี้	(nîi)	*debt*
ห + มา	=	หมา	(mǎa)	*dog*
ห + ยุด	=	หยุด	(yùt)	*to stop*
ห + รีด	=	หรีด	(rìit)	*wreath*
ห + ลาย	=	หลาย	(lǎai)	*several*
ห + วัด	=	หวัด	(wàt)	*cold*

In syllables with the silent high consonant ห, all high consonant tone rules apply. (See pages 103 and 122.)

Tone Mark	Tone Name	Tone	Examples
None	sǐang èek	*low*	หยุด (yùt)
None	sǐang jàt-dtà-waa	*rising*	หมา (mǎa)
่	sǐang èek	*low*	หม่า (màa)
̌	sǐang too	*falling*	หม้า (mâa)

Exercise: Read the Following Words and Practice Writing Them in Thai. Also Identify the Tones.

1. หรือ   *or*   2. โหล   *dozen*

3. หนึ่ง   *one*   4. หมู   *pig*

5. หน้า   *face*   6. หวาน   *sweet*

7. หมอน   *pillow*   8. หลับ   *asleep*

9. หย่า   *to divorce* 10. หงาย   *to lie face up*

Read The Following Aloud

1.   หม่า หม้า หมา

2.   หนี่ หนี้ หนี

3.   หรู่ หรู้ หรู

4.   เหม่ เหม้ เหม

5.   ไหล่ ไหล้ ไหล

6.   เหว่า เหว้า เหวา

7.   หย่อ หย้อ หยอ

8.   โหญ่ โหญ้ โหญ

Writing Exercise 8

Transcribe the following into Thai script using ห นำ
/hɔ̌ɔ-nam/.

1. mìi _____

6. lǎa _____

2. nǎi _____

7. wùu _____

3. yài _____

8. ròng _____

4. nîi _____

9. wàn _____

5. màn _____

10. rǎa _____

Lesson 9

Family and kinship terms; occupations; animals;
how to use ใ; other features of written Thai

bòtîi gâao   บทที่ ๙   *Lesson 9*

kamsàp คำศัพท์ *Vocabulary*

sǔan สวน		*garden*
sǔansàt สวนสัตว์		*zoo*
aa-yú อายุ		*age*
bɔɔ-rí-sàt บริษัท		*company*
tammai ทำไม		*why*
prɔ́/prɔ́-wâa เพราะ/เพราะว่า		*because*
tâa ถ้า		*if*
dtɛ̀ng-ngaan/dtɛ̀ng แต่งงาน/แต่ง		*to get married, to marry*
sòot โสด		*single*
rák รัก		*to love*
táng-sɔ̌ɔng ทั้งสอง		*both*

krɔ̂pkrua ครอบครัว *Family*

pûu-chaai ผู้ชาย		*man, male*
pûu-yǐng ผู้หญิง		*woman, female*
pûu-yài ผู้ใหญ่		*adult*
dèk/lûuk เด็ก/ลูก		*child*
lûukchaai ลูกชาย		*son*
lûuksǎao ลูกสาว		*daughter*
sǎa-mii สามี		*husband*
pan-rá-yaa ภรรยา		*wife*
pǔa ผัว		*husband (colloquial)*
mia เมีย		*wife (colloquial)*
pɔ̂ɔ พ่อ		*father*
mɛ̂ɛ แม่		*mother*
pîi พี่		*older sibling*

nɔ́ɔng น้อง	*younger sibling*
pîi-chaai พี่ชาย	*older brother*
pîi-sǎao พี่สาว	*older sister*
nɔ́ɔng-chaai น้องชาย	*younger brother*
nɔ́ɔng-sǎao น้องสาว	*younger sister*
bpùu ปู่	*father's father*
yâa ย่า	*father's mother*
dtaa ตา	*mother's father*
yaai ยาย	*mother's mother*
lung ลุง	*father or mother's older brother*
bpâa ป้า	*father or mother's older sister*
náa น้า	*mother's younger brother or sister*
aa อา	*father's younger brother or sister*

aa-chîip อาชีพ   *Occupations*

aa-jaan/kruu อาจารย์/ครู	*teacher, professor*
mɔ̌ɔ หมอ	*doctor*
mɔ̌ɔ-fan หมอฟัน	*dentist*
náktú-rá-gìt นักธุรกิจ	*businessman*
náksùk-sǎa นักศึกษา	*college student*
nák-rian นักเรียน	*student*
nák-kǐan นักเขียน	*writer*
nákbin นักบิน	*pilot*
nák-rɔ́ɔng นักร้อง	*singer*
náksùup นักสืบ	*spy*

nák-ɔ̀ɔkbὲɛp	นักออกแบบ	*designer*
kâa-râat-chá-gaan	ข้าราชการ	*government official*
wítsà-wá-gɔɔn	วิศวกร	*engineer*
dtamrùat	ตำรวจ	*policeman*
tá-hǎan	ทหาร	*soldier*
pá-yaa-baan	พยาบาล	*nurse*
kon kàp-rót	คนขับรถ	*driver*
châng	ช่าง	*mechanic*
châng-dtàtpǒm	ช่างตัดผม	*barber*
chaao-naa	ชาวนา	*farmer*
prá	พระ	*monk*
lee-kǎa	เลขา	*secretary*
mɛ̂ɛ-bâan	แม่บ้าน	*housewife*
pɔ̂ɔ-káa/mɛ̂ɛ-káa	พ่อค้า/แม่ค้า	*merchant*
daa-raa	ดารา	*movie star*
jâo-kɔ̌ɔng	เจ้าของ	*owner*
jâo-kɔ̌ɔng-ráan	เจ้าของร้าน	*shop owner*
jâo-kɔ̌ɔng tú-rá-gìt	เจ้าของธุรกิจ	*business owner*
tam-ngaan sùan-dtua	ทำงานส่วนตัว	*self-employed*
tam-ngaan bɔɔ-rí-sàt	ทำงานบริษัท	*company employee*
joon	โจร	*robber*
kà-mooi	ขโมย	*thief*

sàt สัตว์ *Animals*

sàtlíang	สัตว์เลี้ยง	*pet*
dtua-pûu	ตัวผู้	*male (animal)*
dtua-mia	ตัวเมีย	*female (animal)*
mǎa	หมา	*dog*
mɛɛo	แมว	*cat*
mǔu	หมู	*pig*

bpèt เป็ด	duck
gài ไก่	chicken, hen
cháang ช้าง	elephant
máa ม้า	horse
wua วัว	cow, ox
kwaai ควาย	buffalo
bpuu ปู	crab
bplaa ปลา	fish
hɔ̌i หอย	shell, oyster, etc.
gûng กุ้ง	shrimp
nók นก	bird
ling ลิง	monkey
nǔu หนู	rat, mouse
nguu งู	snake
sǔa เสือ	tiger
sǐng-dtoo สิงโต	lion
jɔɔ-rá-kêe จระเข้	crocodile
dtào เต่า	turtle
jîng-jôo จิ้งโจ้	kangaroo
pé แพะ	goat
gè แกะ	sheep
mǐi หมี	bear
ùut อูฐ	camel
káang-kaao ค้างคาว	bat
máa-laai ม้าลาย	zebra
mǎa-bpàa หมาป่า	wolf
mǎa-jîng-jɔ̀ɔk หมาจิ้งจอก	fox
pǐi-sǔa ผีเสื้อ	butterfly
mót มด	ant
yung ยุง	mosquito
má-lɛɛng-wan แมลงวัน	fly

Conversation

Ann: kun jà-ran dtὲng-ngaan rɯ́ yang ká.

แอน: คุณ จรัญ   แต่งงาน   รึ ยัง คะ

Jaran, are you married?

Jaran: dtὲɛng lέɛo kráp. panrá-yaa pǒm chɯ̂ɯ wí-lai.

จรัญ: แต่ง แล้ว ครับ   ภรรยา   ผม   ชื่อ วิไล

Yes. My wife's name is Wilai.

Ann: mii lûuk rɯ́ yang ká.

แอน: มี   ลูก รึ ยัง คะ

Do you have children?

Jaran: mii sɔ̌ɔng kon kráp. pûu-yǐng gàp pûu-chaai.

จรัญ: มี   สอง คน ครับ   ผู้หญิง   กับ ผู้ชาย

I have two, a girl and a boy.

Ann: kun tam-ngaan à-rai ká.

แอน: คุณ   ทำงาน   อะไร คะ

What kind of work do you do?

Jaran: pǒm tam-ngaan tá-naa-kaan kráp.

จรัญ: ผม   ทำงาน   ธนาคาร   ครับ

I work at a bank.

Ann: tá-naa-kaan à-rai ká.

แอน: ธนาคาร   อะไร คะ

What bank?

Jaran: tá-naa-kaan grung-têep kráp.

จรัญ: ธนาคาร   กรุงเทพ ครับ

Bangkok Bank.

kun ɛɛn tam-ngaan à-rai kráp.

คุณ แอน ทำงาน อะไร ครับ

What kind of work do you do, Ann?

Ann: tam-ngaan sùan-dtua tîi à-mee-rí-gaa kâ.

แอน: ทำงาน ส่วนตัว ที่ อเมริกา ค่ะ

I work for myself in America.

Jaran: kun dtèng-ngaan rɯ́ yang kráp.

จรัญ: คุณ แต่งงาน รึ ยัง ครับ

Are you married?

Ann: yang kâ. yang mâi mii fɛɛn.

แอน: ยัง ค่ะ ยัง ไม่ มี แฟน

Not yet. I don't have a boyfriend yet.

bprà-yòok ประโยค *Sentences*

1. A: krɔ̂ɔpkrua kun mii gìi kon.

   ครอบครัว คุณ มี กี่ คน

   How many people are there in your family?

   B: mii jèt kon. kun pɔ̂ɔ, kun mɛ̂ɛ, pîi-chaai, pîi sǎao,

   มี เจ็ด คน คุณ พ่อ คุณ แม่ พี่ชาย พี่สาว

   nɔ́ɔng-chaai sɔ̌ɔng kon gàp dì-chán.

   น้องชาย สอง คน กับ ติฉัน

   There are seven — my father, mother, older brother,
   older sister, two younger brothers and me.

2. A: nân krai.

   นั่น ใคร

   Who is that?

   B: nân nɔ́ɔng-sǎao kɔ̌ɔng pǒm.

   นั่น น้องสาว ของ ผม

   That is my younger sister.

3. A: pîi-chaai kun tam-ngaan à-rai.

   พี่ชาย คุณ ทำงาน อะไร

   What kind of work does your older brother do?

   B: káo bpen wítsà-wá-gɔɔn.

   เขา เป็น วิศวกร

   He is an engineer.

   A: kun tam-ngaan à-rai.

   คุณ ทำงาน อะไร

   What kind of work do you do?

B: pŏm tam-ngaan bɔɔ-rí-sàt.

ผม   ทำงาน   บริษัท

I work for a company.

4. A: káo mii aa-chîip à-rai.

เขา   มี   อาชีพ   อะไร

What is his occupation?

B: káo bpen aa-jaan paa-sǎa tai.

เขา เป็น อาจารย์   ภาษาไทย

He is a Thai teacher.

5. A: kun dtɛ̀ng-ngaan rú yang.

คุณ   แต่งงาน   รึ   ยัง

Are you married yet?

B: dtɛ̀ng lɛ́ɛo.

แต่ง แล้ว

Yes, I am.

C: yang mâi dtɛ̀ng.   yang bpen sòot.

ยัง   ไม่   แต่ง   ยัง   เป็น โสด

No, I'm not. I'm still single.

6. A: kun mii lûuk gìi kon.

คุณ มี ลูก   กี่ คน

How many children do you have?

B: sɔɔng kon.   táng sɔ̌ɔng kon bpen pûu-chaai.

สอง คน   ทั้ง   สอง คน เป็น ผู้ชาย

Two. Both of them are boys.

7. A: kun aa-yú tâo-rài. / kun aa-yú gîi bpii.

คุณ อายุ   เท่าไหร่ / คุณ อายุ กี่ ปี

How old are you?

B: săamsìp bpii.

สามสิบ ปี

Thirty years old.

A: pîi-săao kun aa-yú tâo-rài.

พี่สาว คุณ อายุ เท่าไหร่

How old is your older sister?

B: săamsìpsìi.

สามสิบสี่

Thirty-four.

8. A: bâan kun mii sàtlíang mái.

บ้าน คุณ มี สัตว์เลี้ยง มั้ย

Do you have pets at home?

B: mii. mii măa gàp mɛɛo.

มี มี หมา กับ แมว

Yes, I have a dog and a cat.

9. A: krai bpen kruu paa-săa tai.

ใคร เป็น ครู ภาษาไทย

Who is the Thai teacher?

B: kun sŏmchai bpen kruu paa-săa tai.

คุณ สมชัย เป็น ครู ภาษา ไทย

Mr. Somchai is the Thai teacher.

10. A: kun tam-ngaan gàp bɔɔ-rí-sàt à-rai.

คุณ ทำงาน กับ บริษัท อะไร

What company do you work with?

B: gàp bɔɔ-rí-sàt yîi-bpùn.

กับ บริษัท ญี่ปุ่น

With a Japanese company.

11. A: tammai kun rian paa-sǎa tai.

     ทำไม   คุณ เรียน ภาษา ไทย

     Why do you study Thai?

  B: prɔ́-wâa pǒm chɔ̂ɔp kon tai mâak.

     เพราะว่า ผม   ชอบ   คน ไทย มาก

     Because I like Thai people very much.

12. A: tammai kun mâi maa wát aa-tít tîi-lɛ́ɛo.

     ทำไม   คุณ ไม่ มา วัด อาทิตย์ ที่แล้ว

     Why didn't you come to the temple last week?

  B: prɔ́-wâa mâi kɔ̂i sà-baai.

     เพราะว่า ไม่ ค่อย สบาย

     Because I wasn't feeling well.

13. A: tâa kun mii ngən mâak mâak, kun yàak jà tam à-rai.

     ถ้า คุณ มี เงิน   มากๆ   คุณ อยาก จะ ทำ อะไร

     If you had a lot of money, what would you do?

  B: jà súu bâan tîi mɯang tai.

     จะ ซื้อ บ้าน ที่ เมือง ไทย

     I would buy a house in Thailand.

14. A: tâa fǒn dtòk, kun jà tam yang-ngai.

     ถ้า ฝน ตก   คุณ จะ ทำ   ยังไง

     If it rains, what will you do?

  B: jà mâi bpai tam-ngaan.

     จะ ไม่ ไป   ทำงาน

     I won't go to work.

15.   wanníi bpùat fan mâak, yàak bpai hǎa mɔ̌ɔ-fan.

     วันนี้   ปวด ฟัน มาก อยาก ไป หา หมอฟัน

     Today I have a bad toothache. I want to see a dentist.

16.   dì-chán kít wâa káo bpen nák-tú-rá-gìt jàak yîi-bpùn.

ดิฉัน   คิด   ว่า   เขา   เป็น   นักธุรกิจ   จาก   ญี่ปุ่น

I think he is a businessman from Japan.

17.   tîi-nîi mii kà-mooi mâak jing-jing.

ที่นี่   มี   ขโมย   มาก   จริงๆ

This place really has a lot of thieves.

18. A: pŏm mii lung yùu tîi ang-grìt.

ผม   มี   ลุง   อยู่   ที่   อังกฤษ

I have an uncle in England.

     B: káo mii krɔ̂ɔpkrua yùu tîi mʉang tai.

เขา   มี   ครอบครัว   อยู่   ที่   เมือง   ไทย

He has a family in Thailand.

19. A: pŏm yàak dtɛ̀ng-ngaan gàp kun.

ผม   อยาก   แต่งงาน   กับ   คุณ

I want to marry you.

     B: káo yàak dtɛ̀ng-ngaan gàp kon tai.

เขา อยาก   แต่งงาน   กับ   คน ไทย

He wants to marry a Thai.

20. A: pŏm rák kun mâak.

ผม   รัก   คุณ   มาก

I love you very much.

     B: káo rák krɔ̂ɔpkrua mâak.

เขา รัก   ครอบครัว   มาก

He loves his family very much.

     C: dì-chán rák mʉang tai.

ดิฉัน   รัก   เมือง   ไทย

I love Thailand.

Test 9

Match the English words with the Thai words.

A   Family

_____ 1. *uncle*

_____ 2. *grandfather*

_____ 3. *daughter*

_____ 4. *younger brother*

_____ 5. *grandmother*

_____ 6. *aunt*

_____ 7. *son*

_____ 8. *husband*

_____ 9. *wife*

_____ 10. *older sister*

a. nɔ́ɔng-sǎao   น้องสาว

b. pan-rá-yaa   ภรรยา

c. lung   ลุง

d. lûuksǎao   ลูกสาว

e. bpùu   ปู่

f. sǎa-mii   สามี

g. pîi-chaai   พี่ชาย

h. lûuk-chaai   ลูกชาย

i. mɛ̂ɛ   แม่

j. pîi-sǎao   พี่สาว

k. nɔ́ɔng-chaai   น้องชาย

l. bpâa   ป้า

m. yâa   ย่า

B   Occupations

_____ 1. *dentist*

_____ 2. *soldier*

_____ 3. *nurse*

_____ 4. *farmer*

_____ 5. *movie star*

_____ 6. *police*

_____ 7. *student*

_____ 8. *singer*

_____ 9. *engineer*

_____ 10. *pilot*

a. nákbin   นักบิน

b. wítsà-wá-gɔɔn   วิศวกร

c. pá-yaa-baan   พยาบาล

d. nák-rian   นักเรียน

e. dtamrùat   ตำรวจ

f. nák-rɔ́ɔng   นักร้อง

g. daa-raa   ดารา

h. mɔ̌ɔ-fan   หมอฟัน

i. aa-jaan   อาจารย์

j. tá-hǎan   ทหาร

k. nák-kǐan   นักเขียน

l. chaao-naa   ชาวนา

m. nák-tú-rá-gìt   นักธุรกิจ

C   Animals

_____ 1. *pig*   a. nǔu   หนู
_____ 2. *fish*   b. máa   ม้า
_____ 3. *bird*   c. kǎa   ขา
_____ 4. *horse*   d. gài   ไก่
_____ 5. *monkey*   e. sǔa   เสือ
_____ 6. *tiger*   f. bplaa ปลา
_____ 7. *dog*   g. kwaai ควาย
_____ 8. *shrimp*   h. gûng   กุ้ง
_____ 9. *elephant*   i. mǎa   หมา
_____ 10. *buffalo*   j. ling   ลิง
                           k. mǔu   หมู
                           l. nók   นก
                           m. cháang ช้าง

Translate the following into English.

1. *A:* nɔ́ɔng-chaai kun tam-ngaan à-rai.
      น้องชาย   คุณ   ทำงาน   อะไร
   _____

2.   káo dtɛ̀ng-ngaan gàp kon yîi-bpùn.
      เขา   แต่งงาน   กับ คน ญี่ปุ่น
   _____

3. *A:* tammai kun mâi chɔ̂ɔp aa-hǎan tai.
      ทำไม   คุณ ไม่ ชอบ   อาหาร ไทย
   _____

   B: prɔ́-wâa pèt mâak.
      เพราะว่า เผ็ด มาก
   _____

4.   tâa mâi mii ngən, jà glàp mɯang tai mâi dâai.
      ถ้า ไม่ มี เงิน จะ กลับ เมือง ไทยไม่ ได้
   _____

5.   pǒm kít-wâa káo mii krɔ̂ɔpkrua lɛ́ɛo.
      ผม   คิดว่า เขา มี ครอบครัว แล้ว
   _____

How to Use ใ (sà-rà ai mái-múan-สระไอไม้ม้วน)

ไ (sà-rà ai mái má-lai - สระไอไม้มลาย) is used in most cases to represent the /ai/ sound. The vowel ใ is used only with the following twenty words:

ใกล้	glâi	*near*
ใคร	krai	*who*
ใคร่	krâi	*to have desires*
ใจ	jai	*heart*
ใช่	châi	*yes*
ใช้	chái	*to use*
ใด	dai	*whatsoever*
ใต้	dtâai	*under*
ใน	nai	*in*
ใบ	bai	*leaf*
ใบ้	bâi	*mute person*
ใฝ่	fài	*to have an interest in*
ใย	yai	*web*
สะใภ้	sà-pái	*female relative by marriage*
ใส	sǎi	*clear*
ใส่	sài	*to put*
หลงใหล	long-lǎi	*to be crazy about*
ให้	hâi	*to give*
ใหญ่	yài	*big*
ใหม่	mài	*new*

Other Features of Written Thai

1. A silent ร occurs in some words. You have to memorize how these words are pronounced. There are only a few of them.

Examples:

สร้อย	sôi	*necklace*
จริง	jing	*real*
สร้าง	sâang	*to build*
เสร็จ	sèt	*to finish*
สระ	sà	*pond*
เพชร	pét	*diamond*
เศรษฐกิจ	sèettà-gìt	*economy*
เศรษฐี	sèettĭi	*millionaire*
สรง	sŏng	*to bathe*
สร่าง	sàang	*to subside*
เศร้า	sâo	*melancholy*

2. When you see double รร (rɔɔ หัน), pronounce it as /à/ (อะ) when it is in medial position within a syllable. When รร is in a syllable's final position, it is pronounced as /an/ (อัน).

Examples:

กรรม	gam	*karma*
วรรณ	wan	*caste*
จรรยา	jan-yaa	*ethics*
กรรไกร	gan-grai	*scissors*
สรรพ	sàp	*all kinds of*

3. The mark ` (gaa-ran) makes the letter which appears under it silent.

Examples:

คอมพิวเตอร์	kɔmpú-tɔ̂ɔ	*computer*
ครรภ์	kan	*womb*
อาจารย์	aa-jaan	*teacher*
บัลลังก์	banlang	*throne*
รถยนต์	rótyon	*car*
รถเมล์	rótmee	*bus*

4. The mark ๆ (mái yá-mók - ไม้ยมก), repeats the word or phrase that comes before it.

Examples:

จริงๆ	jing-jing	*really*
ช้าๆ	cháa-cháa	*slowly*
ทุกวันๆ	túkwan-túkwan	*everyday*

5. The letter ฤ is pronounced rú, rí or rɚɚ. The letter ฤๅ is pronounced rɯɯ.

Examples:

ฤทธิ์	rít	*supernatural power*
อังกฤษ	ang-grit	*English*
ฤๅษี	rɯɯ-sǐi	*hermit*
ฤดู	rú-duu	*season*
ฤกษ์	rɚ̂ɚk	*auspicious time*

พฤหัส	pá-rʉ́-hàt	*Thursday*
พฤษภา	prʉ́tsà-paa	*May*
พฤศจิกา	prʉ́tsà-jì-gaa	*November*

6. There are a few words in Thai with the prefix บริ (bɔɔ-rí).

Examples:

บริการ	bɔɔ-rí-gaan	*service*
บริจาค	bɔɔ-rí-jàak	*to donate*
บริโภค	bɔɔ-rí-pôok	*to consume*
บริษัท	bɔɔ-rí-sàt	*company*
บริสุทธิ์	bɔɔ-rí-sùt	*pure*
บริหาร	bɔɔ-rí-hǎan	*to administer*

7. When ท + ร are in initial position, they form one sound which is read as if it were the low consonant ซ (sɔɔ sôo = /s/).

Examples:

ทรวดทรง	sûatsong	*shape*
ทราย	saai	*sand*
ทราบ	sâap	*to know*
ทรัพย์	sáp	*treasure*
ทราม	saam	*disgraceful*

8. When the letter ร is in final position within a syllable and there is no written vowel, the sound of the vowel sound is /ɔɔ/.

The final ร is pronounced as /n/.

Examples:

พร	pɔɔn	*blessing*
นคร	ná-kɔɔn	*city*
ละคร	lá-kɔɔn	*play*
ยโสธร	yá-sŏo-tɔɔn	*Yasothon-a province in Northeast Thailand*

9. Often the short vowel sound ะ (/à/) is unwritten. It is always in the final position within a syllable, but never at the end of a word. (At the end of a word, the ะ is always written out.) The unwritten ะ usually occurs between two consonants which cannot form a consonant cluster.

Examples:

สบาย	sà-baai	*to feel good*
มหาวิทยาลัย	má-hăa-wíttá-yaa-lai	*university*
ธนาคาร	tá-naa-kaan	*bank*
พนัน	pá-nan	*to gamble*

10. When the unwritten ะ is used with a middle or high consonant, and the following syllable starts with a low consonant, the tone rules may be affected. Frequently, the low consonant will take on the tone characteristics of the initial middle or high consonant. In these cases, the word is pronounced as if the low consonant hid a silent ห (for high consonants) or a silent อ (for middle consonants) in front of it.

Examples:

ขนุน	(ข+หนุน)	kà-nŭn	*jackfruit*
สนุก	(ส+หนุก)	sà-nùk	*to have fun*
ถนน	(ถ+หนน)	tà-nŏn	*road*
จมูก	(จ+อมูก)	jà-mùuk	*nose*
ตลาด	(ต+อลาด)	tà-làat	*market*

11. Another common unwritten vowel is โ-ะ (/o/). It always occurs in the medial position within a syllable between two consonants.

Examples:

คน	kon	*person*
นม	nom	*milk*
กบ	gòp	*frog*
มด	mót	*ant*
นก	nók	*bird*
รถยนต์	rótyon	*car*
สนใจ	sŏnjai	*interested*

12. The consonants จ, ช, ญ, ร, ล, ศ, ษ, ส are pronounced one way in initial position and differently in a syllable's final position.

Examples:

<u>จ</u>าก	jàak	กา<u>จ</u>	gàat
<u>ช</u>าร	chaan	รา<u>ช</u>	râat
<u>ร</u>าด	râat	ดา<u>ร</u>	daan
<u>ล</u>าก	lâak	กา<u>ล</u>	gaan

ศาล	sǎan	ลาศ	lâat
ษาด	sàat	ดาษ	dàat
สาก	sàak	กาส	gàat

13. The consonants จ, ช, ล, ศ, ษ, ส can simultaneously function as a final consonant in one syllable and as the initial consonant of the following syllable. Although the consonant is written only once, in these cases it is pronounced twice — in two different ways and in the two different syllables.

Letter	Final Position Sound	Initial Position Sound
จ	t	j
กิจการ	gìtjà-gaan	*business affairs*
ช	t	ch
ราชการ	râatchá-gaan	*official*
ล	n	l
จุลทัศน์	junlá-tát	*microscope*
ศ	t	s
ทัศนาจร	tátsà-naa-jɔɔn	*sightseeing*
ษ	t	s
บุษบา	bùtsà-baa	*Butsaba-a name*
ส	t	s
พิสดาร	pítsà-daan	*peculiar*

14. Written Thai is generally phonetic, but there are exceptions. Here are a few common words in which the vowel length is irregular.

Examples:

น้ำ *(water) is pronounced as /náam/, but* ซ้ำ *(to repeat) is pronounced as /sám/ which is shorter.*

เช้า *(morning) is pronounced as /cháao/, but* เล้า *(animal pen) is pronounced as /láo/ which is shorter.*

ได้ *(to be able to) is pronounced as /dâai/, but* ไกล้ *(near) is pronounced as /glâi/ which is shorter.*

15. The mark ๆ (bpai-yaan-lék - ไปยาลเล็ก) is often used to abbreviate words that are commonly understood and long names of associations, organizations, cities, etc.

Examples:

กรุงเทพฯ *is short for* กรุงเทพมหานคร *(Bangkok).*

พณฯ ท่าน *is short for* พณหัวเจ้าท่าน *(Your Excellency).*

16. The mark ฯลฯ (bpai-yaan-yài - ไปยาลใหญ่) is like "etc." in English. It is generally used at the end of a list to indicate that the list is not all inclusive.

Lesson 10

Comparisons; adjectives; classifiers

bòttîi sìp บทที่ ๑๐ *Lesson 10*

kamsàp คำศัพท์ *Vocabulary*

gwàa กว่า	*than*
tîi-sùt ที่สุด	*most*
dtὲɛ แต่	*but*
yài/dtoo ใหญ่/โต	*big*
lék เล็ก	*small*
uân อ้วน	*fat*
pɔ̌ɔm ผอม	*thin*
nǎa หนา	*thick*
baang บาง	*thin*
sǔung สูง	*tall, high (height)*
dtîa เตี้ย	*short (height)*
dtàm ต่ำ	*low*
yaao ยาว	*long (measurement)*
sân สั้น	*short (measurement)*
nàk หนัก	*heavy*
bao เบา	*light (weight)*
gwâang กว้าง	*wide*
kêɛp แคบ	*narrow*
rɔ́ɔn ร้อน	*hot*
nǎao หนาว	*cold (weather)*
yen เย็น	*cold, cool*
mâak มาก	*much, many*
nɔ́ɔi น้อย	*little*
aa-yú-mâak/gὲɛ อายุมาก/แก่	*old*
aa-yú-nɔ́ɔi อายุน้อย	*young*
mài ใหม่	*new*
gào เก่า	*old*

kĕng-rɛɛng แข็งแรง	*strong*
ɔ̀ɔn-ɛɛ อ่อนแอ	*weak*
chà-làat ฉลาด	*intelligent*
ngôo โง่	*stupid*
sà-wàang สว่าง	*bright, light*
mûut มืด	*dark*
glai ไกล	*far*
glâi ใกล้	*near*
an-dtà-raai อันตราย	*dangerous*
bplɔ̀ɔtpai ปลอดภัย	*safe*
nâa-glua น่ากลัว	*awful, terrifying*
nâa-sŏnjai น่าสนใจ	*interesting*
nâa-bùa น่าเบื่อ	*boring*
sà-dùak สะดวก	*convenient*
sà-baai สบาย	*comfortable*
sà-àat สะอาด	*clean*
sòkgà-bpròk สกปรก	*dirty*
yûng ยุ่ง	*busy*
wâang ว่าง	*free, empty*
kà-yăn ขยัน	*diligent*
kîi-gìat ขี้เกียจ	*lazy*
ruai รวย	*rich*
jon จน	*poor*
sŭai สวย	*beautiful, pretty*
nâa-rák น่ารัก	*cute*
rûup-lɔ̀ɔ/lɔ̀ɔ รูปหล่อ/ หล่อ	*handsome*
mii-chûu-sĭang/dang	*famous*
มีชื่อเสียง/ ดัง	
sămkan สำคัญ	*important*
pí-sèet พิเศษ	*special*

kîi-nǐao ขี้เหนียว	*thrifty, cheap*
dii-jai ดีใจ	*glad*
jai-dii ใจดี	*kind*
jai-gwâang ใจกว้าง	*generous*
jai-yen ใจเย็น	*calm*
jai-rɔ́ɔn ใจร้อน	*impatient*
leeo เลว	*bad*
ngîap เงียบ	*quiet*
kɔ̌ɔ ขอ	*to ask for something*
sùup สูบ	*to smoke*
glìat เกลียด	*to hate*
goo-hòk โกหก	*to lie*
lôok โลก	*earth, world*
raa-kaa ราคา	*price*
gan กัน	*each other*
mǔan-gan เหมือนกัน	*same, to look like*
kláai-gan คล้ายกัน	*to look like*
tâo-gan เท่ากัน	*equal*

Other Helpful Nouns

nâa หน้า	*page*
dtua-nǎngsǔu ตัวหนังสือ	*letter of the alphabet*
dtúk-gà-dtaa ตุ๊กตา	*doll*
bù-rìi บุหรี่	*cigarette*
nít-dtà-yá-sǎan นิตยสาร	*magazine*
mîit มีด	*knife*
tian เทียน	*candle*
kěm เข็ม	*needle*
lûuk-om ลูกอม	*candy*
tîi-kìa-bù-rìi ที่เขี่ยบุหรี่	*ashtray*

gɛ̂ɛo แก้ว	glass
tûai ถ้วย	cup
pǒnlá-máai ผลไม้	fruit
glûai กล้วย	banana
tú-rian ทุเรียน	durian
má-mûang มะม่วง	mango
mang-kút มังคุด	mangosteen
ngɔ́ เงาะ	rambutan
lam-yai ลำใย	longan
má-lá-gɔɔ มะละกอ	papaya
ɛ́p-bpɔ̂n แอปเปิ้ล	apple
nɔ́ɔi-nàa น้อยหน่า	sugar apple
chom-pûu ชมพู่	rose apple
sàp-bpà-rót สับปะรด	pineapple
sôm ส้ม	orange
sôm-oo ส้มโอ	pomelo
kà-nǔn ขนุน	jackfruit
má-práao มะพร้าว	coconut
dtɛɛng-moo แตงโม	watermelon
dɔ̀ɔkmáai ดอกไม้	flower
gù-làap กุหลาบ	rose
glûai-máai กล้วยไม้	orchid
jaan จาน	plate
kùat ขวด	bottle
glɔ̀ng กล่อง	box
kài ไข่	egg
kâao-pàt ข้าวผัด	fried rice
grà-daan กระดาน	board
lûukbɔn/bɔn ลูกบอล/บอล	ball
jòtmǎai จดหมาย	letter

èek-gà-saan เอกสาร	*document*
dtûu-yen ตู้เย็น	*refrigerator*
kɔmpiu-dtɔ̂ə คอมพิวเตอร์	*computer*
chɔ́ɔn ช้อน	*spoon*
sɔ̂m ซ่อม	*fork*
rôm ร่ม	*umbrella*
dtɯ̀k ตึก	*building*
kà-nǒm-bpang ขนมปัง	*bread*
nɯ́a เนื้อ	*meat*
kúkgîi คุกกี้	*cookie*
chán ชั้น	*floor, grade in school*
chá-nít ชนิด	*kind (of things)*
náam-dtaan น้ำตาล	*sugar*
glɯa เกลือ	*salt*
fiim ฟิล์ม	*film*
múantéep ม้วนเทป	*casette tape*
wii-dii-oo วีดีโอ	*video*
sà-dtɛm แสตมป์	*stamp*
daao ดาว	*star*
duang-aa-tít/prá-aa-tít	*sun*
ดวงอาทิตย์/ พระอาทิตย์	
duang-jan/prá-jan	*moon*
ดวงจันทร์/ พระจันทร์	
kɔ̌ɔng-kwǔan ของขวัญ	*present*
tà-nǒn ถนน	*road*
taang-rótfai ทางรถไฟ	*railway*
klɔɔng คลอง	*canal*
nǎng/pâap-pá-yon	*movie*
หนัง/ ภาพยนต์	
rɯ̂ang เรื่อง	*story*

láksà-nà-naam ลักษณนาม *Classifiers*

Classifiers are words which are required in Thai when counting or referring to any concrete noun.

English has similar words. When we say "three glasses of water", "one sheet of paper", "eight head of cattle", the words "glasses", "sheet" and "head" could be called classifiers. Thai, however, uses classifiers much more often than English. It is impossible to speak acceptable Thai without mastering the use of classifiers.

A classifier is generally used with a category of nouns perceived to have a common characteristic. These categories often seem arbitrary. Therefore, it is a good idea to memorize the classifier along with the noun when learning new vocabulary.

Common Classifiers

1. kon (คน) » *people.*
2. dtua (ตัว) » *animals, tables, chairs, shirts, costumes, letters of the alphabet, dolls, cigarettes, etc.*
3. lêm (เล่ม) » *books, notebooks, magazines, knives, candles, needles.*
4. an (อัน) » *pieces of candy, ashtrays, round objects, objects with unknown classifiers.*
5. bai (ใบ) » *glasses, cups, fruits, plates, bottles, boxes, bags, eggs, sheets of paper, containers.*
6. pèn (แผ่น) » *boards, pieces of paper.*
7. lûuk (ลูก) » *fruits, mountains, balls and other round things.*
8. chà-bàp (ฉบับ) » *newspapers, letters, documents.*
9. krûang (เครื่อง) » *radios, T.Vs., refrigerators, computers, electrical or mechanical machines.*
10. lam (ลำ) » *ships, boats, airplanes.*
11. kan (คัน) » *cars, motorcycles, bicycles, spoons, forks, umbrellas, fishing rods.*
12. lǎng (หลัง) » *houses, buildings.*
13. chín (ชิ้น) » *pieces of bread, pieces of meat, cookies, etc.*
14. chán (ชั้น) » *floors of buildings, grades or classes in schools, classes of train or airplane seats.*
15. hôŋng (ห้อง) » *rooms.*
16. dɔ̀ɔk (ดอก) » *flowers.*
17. kráng (ครั้ง) » *times (numbers of occurrences).*
18. yàang (อย่าง) » *kinds of things, numbers of things.*

19. tîi (ที่) » *numbers of dishes, cups, seats.*
20. gɛ̂ɛo (แก้ว) » *numbers of glasses of beer, water, etc.*
21. tûai (ถ้วย) » *numbers of cups of tea, soup, coffee, etc.*
22. kùat (ขวด) » *numbers of bottles of beer, water, etc.*
23. jaan (จาน) » *numbers of plates of rice, food, etc.*
24. gɔ̂ɔn (ก้อน) » *bars of soap, sugar cubes, pieces of candy, etc.*
25. dâam (ด้าม) » *pens.*
26. têng (แท่ง) » *pencils, pieces of chalk.*
27. sên (เส้น) » *threads, neckties, tires, necklaces, bracelets, roads, hairs.*
28. muan (มวน) » *cigarettes.*
29. múan (ม้วน) » *rolls of film, casette tapes, video tapes.*
30. duang (ดวง) » *stamps, stars, suns, moons.*
31. ruan (เรือน) » *clocks, watches.*
32. hɔ̀ɔ (ห่อ) » *presents, bags of sweets, bags of snacks, wrapped things.*
33. sǎai (สาย) » *roads, rivers, canals, railways.*
34. kûu (คู่) » *pairs of things or people.*
35. chút (ชุด) » *sets of things, suits, dresses.*
36. rûang (เรื่อง) » *movies, plays, stories.*
37. dtôn (ต้น) » *trees.*

Notes: 1. *Some nouns can be used with more than one classifier.*
    e.g. glûai sǎam <u>bai</u> *or* glûai sǎam <u>lûuk</u> = *three bananas*
  2. nîi (นี่), nân (นั่น) *and* nôon (โน่น) *which mean 'this', 'that' and 'that' (further) change their tone to* níi (นี้), nán (นั้น) *and* nóon (โน้น) *when they are used as adjectives to modify the classifier.*
    e.g. <u>nîi</u> nǎngsǔu. = *This is a book.*
    nǎngsǔu lêm <u>níi</u> dii. = *This book is good.*

How to Use Classifiers

1. *noun + cardinal number + classifier*

   (one, two, three, ... nùng, sɔ̌ɔng, sǎam)

   e.g. mǎa sǎam <u>dtua</u> = *three dogs*

   pǒm mii mǎa sǎam <u>dtua</u>. = *I have three dogs.*

   nǎngsɯ̌ɯ hâa <u>lêm</u> = *five books*

   nǎngsɯ̌ɯ hâa <u>lêm</u> yùu bon dtó.

   = *Five books are on the table.*

   nùng *is usually replaced with* <u>diao</u> (เดียว) *in normal speech and* <u>diao</u> *is placed after the classifier.*

   e.g. mǎa nùng <u>dtua</u> = mǎa <u>dtua</u> diao *(one dog)*

2. *noun + classifier + n*íi, nán *or* nóon

   e.g. mǎa <u>dtua</u> níi = *this dog*

   mǎa <u>dtua</u> níi sǔai. = *This dog is beautiful.*

   nǎngsɯ̌ɯ <u>lêm</u> nán = *that book*

   nǎngsɯ̌ɯ <u>lêm</u> nán tâo-rài? = *How much is that book?*

3. *noun + classifier + ordinal number*

   (first, second, third, ... tîi nùng, tîi sɔ̌ɔng, tîi sǎam)

   e.g. mǎa <u>dtua</u> tîi nùng = *the first dog*

   mǎa <u>dtua</u> tîi nùng sǐi dam. = *The first dog is black.*

   nǎngsɯ̌ɯ <u>lêm</u> tîi sɔ̌ɔng = *the second book*

   nǎngsɯ̌ɯ <u>lêm</u> tîi sɔ̌ɔng yùu bon dtó

   = *The second book is on the table.*

   tîi nùng *is usually replaced with* <u>rɛ̂ɛk</u> (แรก) *in normal speech.*

   e.g. nǎngsɯ̌ɯ <u>lêm</u> tîi nùng = nǎngsɯ̌ɯ <u>lêm</u> rɛ̂ɛk *(the first book)*

4. *noun +* gìi *+ classifier*

   (asking for the number or amount of something)

e.g. mǎa gìi <u>dtua</u>? = *how many dogs?*
kun mii mǎa gìi <u>dtua</u>.
   = *How many dogs do you have?*
nǎngsǔu gìi <u>lêm</u>. = *how many books?*
káo àan nǎngsǔu gìi <u>lêm</u>.
   = *How many books did he read?*

5. *noun +* <u>*classifier*</u> *+ adjective*
   e.g. mǎa <u>dtua</u> mài = *a new dog*
    pǒm mii mǎa <u>dtua</u> mài. = *I have a new dog.*
    nǎngsǔu <u>lêm</u> gào = *an old book*
    nîi nǎngsǔu <u>lêm</u> gào. = *This is an old book.*

6. *noun +* <u>*classifier*</u> *+* nǎi = *which one.*
   e.g. mǎa <u>dtua</u> nǎi. = *Which dog?*
    kun chɔ̂ɔp mǎa <u>dtua</u> nǎi tîi sùt.
     = *Which dog do you like most?*
    nǎngsǔu <u>lêm</u> nǎi. = *Which book?*
    nǎngsǔu <u>lêm</u> nǎi kɔ̌ɔng kun.
     = *Which one is your book?*

7. *(noun) +* lǎai (หลาย) *+* <u>*classifier*</u> = *many* _____
   e.g. mǎa lǎai dtua *or* lǎai dtua = *many dogs*

Note: When a noun is understood from the context, it is often omitted.
   e.g.   hâa <u>lêm</u> = *five books*
          lêm nîi = *this book*
          lêm rɛ̂ɛk = *the first book*
          gìi <u>lêm</u> = *how many books?*
          lêm gào = *an old book*
          lêm nǎi = *which book?*

Conversation

John: grà-bpǎo bai nán tâo-rài kráp.

จอห์น: กระเป๋า ใบ นั้น เท่าไหร่ ครับ

How much is that bag?

Konkǎai: hâa rɔ́ɔi bàat kâ.

คนขาย: ห้า ร้อย บาท ค่ะ

It's five hundred baht.

John: bai níi là kráp.

จอห์น: ใบ นี้ ล่ะ ครับ

What about this one?

Konkǎai: bai nán sǎam rɔ́ɔi hâa sìp.

คนขาย: ใบ นั้น สาม ร้อย ห้า สิบ

That one is three hundred and fifty.

John: kun mii gìi sǐi kráp.

จอห์น: คุณ มี กี่ สี ครับ

How many colors do you have?

Konkǎai: mii lǎai sǐi kâ.

คนขาย: มี หลาย สี ค่ะ

Many colors.

kun chɔ̂ɔp sǐi à-rai mâak tîi-sùt ká.

คุณ ชอบ สี อะไร มาก ที่สุด คะ

What color do you like the most?

John: chɔ̂ɔp sǐi dam tîi-sùt kráp.

จอห์น: ชอบ สี ดำ ที่สุด ครับ

I like black the most.

kɔ̌ɔ duu bai sǐi dam gàp bai sǐi kǎao.

ขอ ดู ใบ สี ดำ กับ ใบ สี ขาว

May I see the black and the white ones?

Konkǎai: nîi kâ.

คนขาย: นี่ ค่ะ

Here you are.

John: pǒm kít wâa chɔ̂ɔp sǐi dam mâak gwàa.

จอห์น: ผม คิด ว่า ชอบ สี ดำ มาก กว่า

I think I like black better.

tâo-rài ná kráp.

เท่าไหร่ นะ ครับ

How much is it again?

Konkǎai: hâa rɔ́ɔi kâ.

คนขาย: ห้า ร้อย ค่ะ

Five hundred.

John: sìi rɔ́ɔi dâai mái

จอห์น: สี่ ร้อย ได้ ไหม

Can you make it four hundred?

Konkǎai: mâi dâai kâ. sìi rɔ́ɔi hâa-sip gɔ̂ɔ-lɛ́ɛo-gan.

คนขาย: ไม่ ได้ ค่ะ สี่ ร้อย ห้าสิบ ก็แล้วกัน

No, I can't. Let's make it four hundred and fifty.

Note: gɔ̂ɔ-lɛ́ɛo-gan is an expression which urges agreement, such as: let's, you might (do such and such), go ahead, that's it, or that's all there is to it.

bprà-yòok ประโยค *Sentences*

1. A: káo sǔung gwàa pǒm.
    เขา สูง กว่า ผม
    He is taller than I.

    B: nǎngsǔu lêm níi pɛɛng gwàa lêm nán.
    หนังสือ เล่ม นี้ แพง กว่า เล่ม นั้น
    This book is more expensive than that one.

    C: an níi dii gwàa.
    อัน นี้ ดี กว่า
    This one is better.

    D: an-nán sǔai gwàa.
    อัน นั้น สวย กว่า
    That one is more beautiful.

2. A: káo sǔung tîi-sùt nai hɔ̂ng.
    เขา สูง ที่สุด ใน ห้อง
    He is the tallest in the room.

    B: nǎngsǔu lêm níi pɛɛng tîi-sùt.
    หนังสือ เล่ม นี้ แพง ที่สุด
    This book is the most expensive.

    C: an níi dii tîi-sùt.
    อัน นี้ ดี ที่สุด
    This is the best.

    D: an nán sǔai tîi-sùt.
    อัน นั้น สวย ที่สุด
    That one is the most beautiful.

3. A: káo gàp kun kon nǎi sǔung gwàa gan.
    เขา กับ คุณ คน ไหน สูง กว่า กัน
    Who is taller between him and you?

    B: káo sǔung gwàa (pǒm).
    เขา สูง กว่า (ผม)
    He is taller (than I).

A: nǎngsǔu lêm níi gàp lêm nán

หนังสือ เล่ม นี้ กับ เล่ม นั้น

  lêm nǎi pɛɛng gwàa gan.

  เล่ม ไหน แพง กว่า กัน

  Between this book and that book,

  which one is more expensive?

B: nǎngsǔu lêm níi pɛɛng gwàa (lêm nán).

  หนังสือ เล่ม นี้ แพง กว่า (เล่มนั้น)

  This book is more expensive (than that one).

A: an nǎi dii gwàa.

  อัน ไหน ดี กว่า

  Which one is better?

B: an níi dii gwàa.

  อัน นี้ ดี กว่า

  This one is better.

A: an nǎi sǔai gwàa.

  อัน ไหน สวย กว่า

  Which one is more beautiful?

B: an nán sǔai gwàa.

  อัน นั้น สวย กว่า

  That one is more beautiful.

4. A: A yài gwàa B, dtɛ̀ɛ C yài tîi-sùt.

  A ใหญ่ กว่า B   แต่ C ใหญ่ ที่สุด

  A is bigger than B, but C is the biggest.

  B: pǒm chɔ̂ɔp sǐi kǎao mâak gwàa sǐi dam,

  ผม ชอบ สี ขาว มาก กว่า สี ดำ

  dtɛ̀ɛ chɔ̂ɔp sǐi fáa mâak tîi-sùt.

  แต่ ชอบ สี ฟ้า มาก ที่สุด

  I like white more than black, but I like blue the most.

5. A: krûangbin lam níi yài tîi-sùt nai lôok.

  เครื่องบิน ลำ นี้ ใหญ่ ที่สุด ใน โลก

  This airplane is the biggest in the world.

B: pǒm sǔung tîi-sùt nai bâan.

ผม สูง ที่สุด ใน บ้าน

I am the tallest in the house.

C: káo ruai tîi-sùt nai muang tai.

เขา รวย ที่สุด ใน เมือง ไทย

He is the richest in Thailand.

6. A: an níi gàp an nán mǔan-gan.

อัน นี้ กับ อัน นั้น เหมือนกัน

This one and that one are the same.

(Literally: This one and that one look like each other.)

B: sɔ̌ɔng kon nán kláai-gan.

สอง คน นั้น คล้ายกัน

Those two people look alike.

C: nǎngsʉ̌ʉ sɔ̌ɔng lêm níi raa-kaa tâo-gan.

หนังสือ สอง เล่ม นี้ ราคา เท่ากัน

The price of these two books is the same.

7. káo rák gan mâak.

เขา รัก กัน มาก

They love each other very much.

8. káo glìat kun prɔ́   kun chɔ̂ɔp goo-hòk.

เขา เกลียด คุณ เพราะ คุณ ชอบ โกหก

He hates you because you often lie.

(Literally: ... because you like to lie.)

9. A: bâan kun mii sàtlíang mái?

บ้าน คุณ มี สัตว์เลี้ยง ไหม

Do you have pets at home?

B: mii. mii mɛɛo sɔ̌ɔng dtua.

มี มี แมว สอง ตัว

Yes. I have two cats.

The following sentences demonstrate how to use different classifiers. The underlined words are classifiers.

10.   mii kon hâa <u>kon</u> yùu nai hɔ̂ng.
       มี คน ห้า คน อยู่ ใน ห้อง
       There are five people in the room.

11.   sûa <u>dtua</u> níi mâi pɛɛng.
       เสื้อ ตัว นี้ ไม่ แพง
       This shirt is not expensive.

12.   krai kǐan nǎngsǔu <u>lêm</u> nán.
       ใคร เขียน หนังสือ เล่ม นั้น
       Who wrote that book?

13.   kun chɔ̂ɔp <u>an</u> nǎi tîi-sùt.
       คุณ ชอบ อัน ไหน ที่สุด
       Which one do you like the best?

14.   grà-bpǎo <u>bai</u> níi mâi kɔ̂i dii.
       กระเป๋า ใบ นี้ ไม่ ค่อย ดี
       This bag is not very good.

15.   grà-dàat <u>pèn</u> nán baang mâak.
       กระดาษ แผ่น นั้น บาง มาก
       This piece of paper is very thin.

16.   wanníi gin glûai sɔ̌ɔng <u>lûuk</u>.
       วันนี้ กิน กล้วย สอง ลูก
       Today I ate two bananas.

17.   mûa-waanníi kun àan nǎngsǔu-pim gìi <u>chà-bàp</u>.
       เมื่อวานนี้ คุณ อ่าน หนังสือพิมพ์ กี่ ฉบับ
       How many newspapers did you read yesterday?

18.   pǒm mii tii-wii sǎam <u>krûang</u>, kɔmpíu-dtɔ̂ə <u>krûang</u> diao.
       ผม มี ทีวี สาม เครื่อง คอมพิวเตอร์ เครื่อง เดียว
       I have three televisions and one computer.

19.   krûang-bin <u>lam</u> níi maa jàak grung-têep.
       เครื่องบิน ลำ นี้ มา จาก กรุงเทพ
       This airplane came from Bangkok.

20.	rót <u>kan</u> níi tam nai yîi-bpùn.
	รถ <u>คัน</u> นี้ ทำ ใน ญี่ปุ่น
	This car is made in Japan.

21.	pǒm súu bâan <u>lǎng</u> mài.
	ผม ซื้อ บ้าน <u>หลัง</u> ใหม่
	I bought a new house.

22.	núa <u>chín</u> níi à-rɔ̀i jing-jing.
	เนื้อ <u>ชิ้น</u> นี้ อร่อย จริงๆ
	This piece of meat is really delicious.

23.	pǒm yùu <u>chán</u> tîi sǎam.
	ผม อยู่ <u>ชั้น</u> ที่ สาม
	I live on the third floor.

24.	bâan káo mii hɔ̂ng-nɔɔn sìi <u>hɔ̂ng</u>.
	บ้าน เขา มี ห้องนอน สี่ <u>ห้อง</u>
	His house has four bedrooms.

25.	dɔ̀ɔkmáai <u>dɔ̀ɔk</u> níi sǔai mâak.
	ดอกไม้ <u>ดอก</u> นี้ สวย มาก
	This flower is very beautiful.

26.	dì-chán kəəi bpai mɯang tai hâa <u>kráng</u>.
	ดิฉัน เคย ไป เมือง ไทย ห้า <u>ครั้ง</u>
	I have been to Thailand five times.

27.	mii aa-hǎan hòk <u>yàang</u> yùu bon dtó.
	มี อาหาร หก <u>อย่าง</u> อยู่ บน โต๊ะ
	There are five kinds of food on the table.

28.	kɔ̌ɔ kâao nùng <u>tîi</u>.
	ขอ ข้าว หนึ่ง <u>ที่</u>
	Give me one (plate of) rice.

29.	kɔ̌ɔ náam yen sɔ̌ɔng <u>gɛ̂ɛo</u>.
	ขอ น้ำ เย็น สอง <u>แก้ว</u>
	Give me two glasses of cold water.

30.   kɔ̌ɔ gaa-fɛɛ rɔ́ɔn sǎam <u>tûai</u>.

ขอ   กาแฟ   ร้อน สาม <u>ถ้วย</u>

Give me three cups of hot coffee.

31.   kɔ̌ɔ bia   sìi <u>kùat</u>.

ขอ เบียร์ สี่ <u>ขวด</u>

Give me four bottles of beer.

32.   kɔ̌ɔ kâao-pàt hâa <u>jaan</u>.

ขอ   ข้าวผัด   ห้า <u>จาน</u>

Give me five plates of fried rice.

33.   kɔ̌ɔ náam-dtaan hòk <u>gɔ̂ɔn</u>.

ขอ   น้ำตาล   หก   <u>ก้อน</u>

Give me six cubes of sugar.

34. A: kun mii bpàakgaa gìi <u>dâam</u>.

คุณ มี   ปากกา   กี่ <u>ด้าม</u>

How many pens do you have?

B: mii sɔ̌ɔng dâam.

มี   สอง   <u>ด้าม</u>

I have two.

A: kun mii dinsɔ̌ɔ gìi <u>tɛ̂ng</u>.

คุณ มี   ดินสอ กี่ <u>แท่ง</u>

How many pencils do you have?

B: mii tɛ̂ng diao.

มี   <u>แท่ง</u> เดียว

I have one.

35.   sɔ̂i <u>sên</u> níi tâo-rài.

สร้อย <u>เส้น</u> นี้ เท่าไหร่

How much is this necklace?

36.   káo sùup bù-rìi wan lá sìp <u>muan</u>.

เขา สูบ บุหรี่ วัน ละ สิบ <u>มวน</u>

He smokes ten cigarettes a day.

37. rao gamlang duu wii-dii-oo <u>múan</u> tîi sǎam.

เรา กำลัง ดู วีดีโอ <u>ม้วน</u> ที่ สาม

We are watching the third video.

38. pǒm sɯ́ɯ sà-dtɛm yîi-sìp <u>duang</u>.

ผม ซื้อ แสตมป์ ยี่สิบ <u>ดวง</u>

I bought twenty stamps.

39. káo mii na-lí-gaa <u>rɯan</u> mài.

เขา มี นาฬิกา <u>เรือน</u> ใหม่

He has a new watch.

40. mɛ̂ɛ sɯ́ɯ kà-nǒm sìi <u>hɔ̀ɔ</u>.

แม่ ซื้อ ขนม สี่ <u>ห่อ</u>

Mother bought four packages of snacks.

41. mɛ̂ɛ-náam <u>sǎai</u> níi yaao mâak.

แม่น้ำ <u>สาย</u> นี้ ยาว มาก

This river is very long.

42. rɔɔng-táao <u>kûu</u> nán sǔai tîi-sùt.

รองเท้า <u>คู่</u> นั้น สวย ที่สุด

That pair of shoes is the prettiest.

43. nǎngsɯ̌ɯ <u>chút</u> níi nâa-sǒnjai.

หนังสือ <u>ชุด</u> นี้ น่าสนใจ

This set of books is interesting.

44. mɯ̂a-kɯɯn-níi duu nǎng sǎam <u>rɯ̂ang</u>.

เมื่อคืนนี้ ดู หนัง สาม <u>เรื่อง</u>

Last night I watched three movies.

45. dtônmáai <u>dtôn</u> nán aa-yú mâak gwàa pan bpii.

ต้นไม้ <u>ต้น</u> นั้น อายุ มาก กว่า พัน ปี

That tree is more than a thousand years old.

Test 10

Matching

A   Adjectives

_____ 1. *tall*

_____ 2. *new*

_____ 3. *fat*

_____ 4. *cold*

_____ 5. *intelligent*

_____ 6. *small*

_____ 7. *far*

_____ 8. *busy*

_____ 9. *rich*

_____ 10. *special*

a. lék   เล็ก

b. glai   ไกล

c. sǔung   สูง

d. nàk   หนัก

e. nǎao   หนาว

f. yûng   ยุ่ง

g. pí-sèet   พิเศษ

h. ruai   รวย

i. ûan   อ้วน

j. glâi   ใกล้

k. chà-làat   ฉลาด

l. mài   ใหม่

m. jon   จน

B   Nouns

_____ 1. *cigarette*

_____ 2. *magazine*

_____ 3. *letter*

_____ 4. *meat*

_____ 5. *plate*

_____ 6. *sugar*

_____ 7. *movie*

_____ 8. *story*

_____ 9. *building*

_____ 10. *star*

a. nǎng   หนัง

b. kùat   ขวด

c. jaan   จาน

d. núa   เนื้อ

e. jòtmǎai   จดหมาย

f. dtùk   ตึก

g. daao   ดาว

h. nít-dtà-yá-sǎan   นิตยสาร

i. glɯa   เกลือ

j. rɯ̂ang   เรื่อง

k. bù-rìi   บุหรี่

l. chɔ́ɔn   ช้อน

m. náam-dtaan   น้ำตาล

C   Classifiers

Match the following nouns with their proper classifiers.

_____ 1. mǎa   หมา   a. bai   ใบ

_____ 2. rótyon   รถยนต์   b. tɛ̂ng   แท่ง

_____ 3. nǎngsɯ̌ɯ-pim   หนังสือพิมพ์   c. dâam   ด้าม

_____ 4. krɯ̂angbin   เครื่องบิน   d. kan   คัน

_____ 5. kùat   ขวด   e. krɯ̂ang   เครื่อง

_____ 6. bâan   บ้าน   f. sǎai   สาย

_____ 7. tii-wii   ทีวี   g. dtua   ตัว

_____ 8. dinsɔ̌ɔ   ดินสอ   h. lam   ลำ

_____ 9. tîi-kìa-bù-rìi   ที่เขี่ยบุหรี่   i. rɯan   เรือน

_____ 10. tà-nǒn   ถนน   j. pɛ̀n   แผ่น

                                      k. lǎng   หลัง

                                      l. an   อัน

                                      m. chà-bàp   ฉบับ

Translate the following into English.

1. A: má-mûang lûuk nǎi à-rɔ̀i tîi-sùt.
    มะม่วง   ลูก ไหน อร่อย ที่สุด

    _____

    B: kít wâa lûuk níi à-rɔ̀i tîi-sùt.
    คิด ว่า ลูก นี้ อร่อย ที่สุด

    _____

2. A: bâan kun mii gìi chán.   B: mii sǎam chán.
    บ้าน คุณ มี กี่ ชั้น   มี สาม ชั้น

    _____

3. A: rɯa lam rɛ̂ɛk jà maa mɯ̂a-rài.
    เรือ ลำ แรก จะ มา เมื่อไหร่

    _____

    B: jà maa prûng-níi.
    จะ มา พรุ่งนี้

    _____

4. mɯ̂a-waanníi sɯ́ɯ naa-lí-gaa rɯan mài.
    เมื่อวานนี้ ซื้อ นาฬิกา เรือน ใหม่

    _____

5. tîi sǔansàt mii cháang hâa dtua.
    ที่ สวนสัตว์ มี ช้าง ห้า ตัว

    _____

Reading Exercise

Read the following aloud and translate.

A.

1. คุณ ชื่อ อะไร

2. ภาษาไทย ไม่ ยาก

3. ผม ชอบ สีขาว

4. เขา มี บ้าน สวยๆ

5. คุณ สบายดี ไหม

6. ดิฉัน เป็น คนไทย

7. อันนี้ เท่าไหร่

8. คุณทานากะ เป็น คนญี่ปุ่น

9. ห้องน้ำ อยู่ ที่ไหน

10. ดินสอ อยู่ ใต้ เก้าอี้

11. โรงแรม อยู่ ทางขวา

12. คนนั้น สวย จริงๆ

13. วันนี้ วัน อะไร

14. วันนี้ วัน อาทิตย์

15. รถยนต์ ของ คุณ สี อะไร

16. ผม ไป โรงเรียน ตอน เช้า

17. คุณ สมชาย ชอบ ดู ทีวี

18. เรา จะไป กิน อาหารไทย

19. ตอนนี้ เวลา เท่าไหร่

20. จะไป สนามบิน ตอน หก ทุ่ม

B.

1. คุณ จะ ไป ไหน

2. จะ ไป เรียน ภาษาไทย

3. ผม ไม่ ชอบ อาหารฝรั่ง

4. เขา มี หมา ที่ บ้าน

5. ผม จะไป เมือง ไทย เดือน หน้า

6. วันจันทร์หน้า ผม จะ ไม่ อยู่

7. เรา จะไป เรียน ภาษาอังกฤษ ที่ อเมริกา

8. คน ญี่ปุ่น ชอบ ทำงาน

9. ผม อยาก ไป ห้องน้ำ

10. คุณ กำลัง ทำ อะไร

11. คุณจอห์น พูด ภาษาจีน ได้

12. วันนี้ เหนื่อย จริงๆ

13. นี่ หนังสือ ของ ใคร

14. วันนี้ ร้อน มาก

15. แฟน คุณ ชื่อ อะไร

16. ผม อาบน้ำ ทุก วัน

17. ดิฉัน ซักผ้า ทุก วันเสาร์

18. เรา ไม่ อยาก ซื้อ ของ แพง

19. ตอนนี้ ปวดหัว มาก

20. ผม แปรงฟัน วันละ สอง ครั้ง

C.

1. อเมริกา ใหญ่ กว่า เมือง ไทย

2. รถ คัน นั้น สวย ที่ สุด

3. ผม ชอบ สี ขาว มากกว่า สี ดำ

4. เขา มี หมา สาม ตัว

5. ลูกชาย ผม อยาก จะ เป็น นักบิน

6. คุณ มี พี่ น้อง กี่ คน

7. พี่ สาว คุณ ทำงาน อะไร

8. ทำไม คน ญี่ปุ่น ชอบ ทำงาน

9. ดิฉัน อยาก มี ลูก สอง คน

10. เมื่อวานนี้ ผม ซื้อ รองเท้า สี่ คู่

11. คุณแดง พูด ภาษา อังกฤษ ไม่ ค่อย ถูก

12. ทำไม คุณ ไม่ ไป ทำงาน

13. คุณ อายุ เท่าไหร่

14. ผม เป็น นัก ธุรกิจ

15. เขา มี แฟน หลาย คน

16. ผม กำลัง แต่งตัว

17. ดิฉัน ซักผ้า ทุก วัน

18. พรุ่งนี้ จะ ไป ตัด ผม

19. มี ธุระ มาก จริงๆ

20. ถ้า คุณ มี เงิน มากๆ คุณ อยาก จะ ทำ อะไร

D.

1. วันนี้ ไม่ ค่อย สบาย

2. พรุ่งนี้ ผม ไป เที่ยว ไม่ ได้ เลย

3. เรียน ภาษา ไทย สนุก ดี

4. ผู้ชาย คน นั้น ชอบ อ่าน หนังสือ

5. ห้องน้ำ ผู้หญิง อยู่ ที่ไหน

6. คุณแนน อยู่ บน ชั้น สอง

7. ผม ชอบ อ่าน หนังสือพิมพ์ ภาษา อังกฤษ

8. เดี๋ยวนี้ เขา ไม่ ค่อย ไป เรียน ภาษา ไทย
    ที่ วัด

9. ร้านอาหาร อยู่ ใกล้ กับ โรงแรม ดุสิต

10. ผม หิว ข้าว มาก เพราะว่า ไม่ ได้ กิน
    ข้าว เช้า

11. ทำไม คน นั้น ไม่ อยาก ไป เที่ยว กับ เรา

12. เขา บอก ว่า กิน ไม่ ได้ เพราะว่า เผ็ด มาก

13. น้องชาย ดิฉัน ไม่ ชอบ อ่าน หนังสือพิมพ์
    แต่ ชอบ ดู ทีวี

14. เขา เป็น นักธุรกิจ ที่ เก่ง จริงๆ

15. บ้าน หลัง นี้ กับ หลัง นั้น หลัง ไหน
สวย กว่า กัน

16. บ้าน คุณ มี สัตว์เลี้ยง ไหม

17. เรา ขาย อาหาร ที่ อเมริกา เมือง แอลเอ

18. อาทิตย์ ที่แล้ว เรา ไป เที่ยว สวนสัตว์

19. ครอบครัว ของ ผม มี ห้า คน

20. คุณ เล็ก เป็น ข้าราชการ ที่ เมือง ไทย

E.　น้อยเป็นนักศึกษาที่มหาวิทยาลัยขอนแก่น

กำลังเรียนวิชาภาษาอังกฤษเป็นวิชาเอก

ปีหน้าน้อยอยากจะมาเรียนที่อเมริกา

น้อยมีพี่ชายทำงานที่แอลเอ

F.　เมื่อวานนี้ผมไปซื้อของที่สีลม

ซื้อรองเท้ามาหนึ่งคู่　กระเป๋าสองใบ

หนังสือสามเล่ม　ปากกาสี่ด้าม　ดินสอห้าแท่ง

เสื้อยืดหกตัว　และเข็มขัดเจ็ดเส้น

Appendix I
Summary of the Thai Writing System

Summary of the
Thai Writing System

The 44 Thai Consonants in
Alphabetical Order

Consonant	Consonant Name	Sound
ก	ก ไก่ gɔɔ gài *(chicken)*●	/g/
ข	ข ไข่ kɔ̌ɔ kài *(egg)*❖	/k/
ฃ	ฃ ขวด kɔ̌ɔ kùat *(bottle)*❖	/k/
ค	ค ควาย kɔɔ kwaai *(buffalo)*	/k/
ฅ	ฅ คน kɔɔ kon *(person)*	/k/
ฆ	ฆ ระฆัง kɔɔ rá-kang *(bell)*	/k/
ง	ง งู ngɔɔ nguu *(snake)*	/ng/
จ	จ จาน jɔɔ jaan *(plate)*●	/j/
ฉ	ฉ ฉิ่ง chɔ̌ɔ chìng *(small cymbal)*❖	/ch/
ช	ช ช้าง chɔɔ cháang *(elephant)*	/ch/

ซ	ซ โซ่	sɔɔ sôo *(chain)*	/s/
ฌ	ฌ เฌอ	chɔɔ chəə *(a kind of tree)*	/ch/
ญ	ญ หญิง	yɔɔ yǐng *(woman)*	/y/
ฎ	ฎ ชะฎา	dɔɔ chá-daa *(a kind of crown)*✿	/d/
ฏ	ฏ ปะฏัก	dtɔɔ bpà-dtàk *(a kind of spear)*✿	/dt/
ฐ	ฐ ฐาน	tɔ̌ɔ tǎan *(base)*❖	/t/
ฑ	มณโฑ	tɔɔ montoo *(Montho the Queen)*	/t/
ฒ	ฒ ผู้เฒ่า	tɔɔ pûu-tâʋ *(old man)*	/t/
ณ	ณ เณร	nɔɔ neen *(young monk)*	/n/
ด	ด เด็ก	dɔɔ dèk *(child)*✿	/d/
ต	ต เต่า	dtɔɔ dtào *(turtle)*✿	/dt/
ถ	ถ ถุง	tɔ̌ɔ tǔng *(bag)*❖	/t/
ท	ท ทหาร	tɔɔ tá-hǎan *(soldier)*	/t/
ธ	ธ ธง	tɔɔ tong *(flag)*	/t/

น	น หนู	nɔɔ nǔu *(mouse)*	/n/
บ	บ ใบไม้	bɔɔ bai-máai *(leaf)*●	/b/
ป	ป ปลา	bpɔɔ bplaa *(fish)*●	/bp/
ผ	ผ ผึ้ง	pɔ̌ɔ pʉ̂ng *(bee)*❖	/p/
ฝ	ฝ ฝา	fɔ̌ɔ fǎa *(lid)*❖	/f/
พ	พ พาน	pɔɔ paan *(tray)*	/p/
ฟ	ฟ ฟัน	fɔɔ fan *(tooth)*	/f/
ภ	ภ สำเภา	pɔɔ sǎmpao *(a kind of ship)*	/p/
ม	ม ม้า	mɔɔ máa *(horse)*	/m/
ย	ย ยักษ์	yɔɔ yák *(giant)*	/y/
ร	ร เรือ	rɔɔ rʉa (boat)	/r/
ล	ล ลิง	lɔɔ ling *(monkey)*	/l/
ว	ว แหวน	wɔɔ wɛ̌ɛn *(ring)*	/w/
ศ	ศ ศาลา	sɔ̌ɔ sǎa-laa *(pavilion)*❖	/s/

ษ	ษ ฤๅษี	sɔ̌ɔ rɯɯ-sǐi *(hermit)*❖	/s/
ส	ส เสือ	sɔ̌ɔ sǔa *(tiger)*❖	/s/
ห	ห หีบ	hɔ̌ɔ hìip *(a kind of box)*❖	/h/
ฬ	ฬ จุฬา	lɔɔ jù-laa *(a kind of kite)*	/l/
อ	อ อ่าง	ɔɔ àang *(basin)*✿	/ɔ/
ฮ	ฮ นกฮูก	hɔɔ nókhûuk (owl)	/h/

❖   = high consonant (11 out of 44)
✿   = middle consonant (9 out of 44)
No mark = low consonant (24 out of 44)

Note: Every Thai consonant has a name which distiguishes it
        from other consonants with the same sound   Since these
        names are standardized and universal, you can always tell
        Thai people how to spell a word without having to
        actually show them

Vowels (sàrà - สระ)

1.	$-\overset{\circ}{\smile}$ /à/		$-$ า	/aa/
2.	$\overset{\frown}{-}$ /ĭ/		$\overset{\frown}{=}$	/ii/
3.	$\overset{\frown}{-}$ /ǔ/		$\overset{\frown}{-}$ อ	/ʉʉ/
4.	$\overset{}{-}_{\,ุ}$ /ù/		$-_{\,ู}$	/uu/
5.	เ$-\overset{\circ}{\smile}$ /è/		เ$-$	/ee/
6.	แ$-\overset{\circ}{\smile}$ /ɛ̀/		แ$-$	/ɛɛ/
7.	โ$-\overset{\circ}{\smile}$ /ò/		โ$-$	/oo/
8.	เ$-$ าะ /ɔ̀/		$-$ อ	/ɔɔ/
9.	$-\overset{\circ}{\smile}$ วะ /ùa/		$-\overset{\circ}{\smile}$ ว	/ua/
10.	เ$-$ ียะ /ĭa/		เ$-$ ีย	/ia/
11.	เ$-$ ือะ /ǔa/		เ$-$ ือ	/ʉa/
12.	เ$-$ อะ /ə̀/		เ$-$ อ	/əə/

Notes: 1. *1-12 on the left are short vowels and their counterparts (long vowels) are on the right.*

2. *9-11 are diphthongs.*

Some of the following vowels may sound either short or long, but they are categorized as long vowels for tone rule purposes.

◌ํา (am)

ใ− (ai   mái-múan)

ไ− (ai mái-má-lai)

เ−า (ao)

เ−ย (ɔɔi)

Tone Marks

Thai has four tone marks.

Tone Mark	Name

ı
— mái èek (ไม้เอก)
ย
— mái too (ไม้โท)
ด
— mái dtrii (ไม้ศรี)
+
— mái jàt-dtà-waa (ไม้จัตวา)

'mái' (ไม้) refers to the tone mark, not to the tone sound of the syllable in which it occurs. 'mái dtrii' and 'mái jàt-dtà-waa' can be used with middle consonants only.

Tone Names

Many Thai syllables have no tone mark at all. Every syllable in Thai is pronounced with one of the five tones, however, and each of these tone sounds has a name as follows:

Tone	Tone Name	
Mid Tone	sĭang sǎa-man	(เสียงสามัญ)
Low Tone	sĭang èek	(เสียงเอก)
Falling Tone	sĭang too	(เสียงโท)
High Tone	sĭang dtrii	(เสียงศรี)
Rising	sĭang jàt-dtà-waa	(เสียงจัตวา)

'sĭang' (เสียง) refers to the actual tone sound, not to the tone marks or tone rules that may be used in the syllable.

While the tone names are similar to the tone mark names, they do not refer to the same thing. For example, the tone mark 'mái èek' (ไม้เอก) may generate the tone sound 'sĭang too' (เสียงโท) depending on the consanant class.

Other Punctuation Marks

−ๆ   mái yá-mók (ไม้ยมก)

−ั   mái hăn-aa-gàat (ไม้หันอากาศ)

−็   mái dtài-kúu (ไม้ไต่คู้)

−์   gaa-ran (การันต์)

ๆ   bpai-yaan-nɔ́ɔi (ไปยาลน้อย)

ๆลๆ   bpai-yaan-yài (ไปยาลใหญ่)

!   àtsà-jee-rii (อัศเจรีย์)

?   bpràtsà-nii (ปรัศนีย์)

<u>Numbers</u>

๐	ศูนย์	0
๑	หนึ่ง	1
๒	สอง	2
๓	สาม	3
๔	สี่	4
๕	ห้า	5
๖	หก	6
๗	เจ็ด	7
๘	แปด	8
๙	เก้า	9

Final Consonants

There are eight basic final consonant sounds: three stop and five sonorant finals as follows:

Sonorant Finals

ง	ง งู	ngɔɔ nguu *(snake)*	/ng/
น	น หนู	nɔɔ nǔu *(mouse)*	/n/
ม	ม ม้า	mɔɔ máa *(horse)*	/m/
ย	ย ยักษ์	yɔɔ yák *(giant)*	/y/
ว	ว แหวน	wɔɔ wěɛn *(ring)*	/w/

Stop Finals

ก	ก ไก่	gɔɔ gài *(chicken)**	/k/
ค	ค เด็ก	dɔɔ dèk *(child)**	/t/
บ	บ ใบไม้	bɔɔ bai-máai *(leaf)**	/p/

Notes: 1. When ก, ค, บ and ย are initial consonants, they are transcribed as /g-/, /d-/, /b-/ and /y-/ respectively. However, when they are final consonants, they are transcribed as /-k/, /-t/, /-p/ and /-i/.

2. ว forms part of the vowels ◌ัวะ and ◌ัว, which are transcribed as /ùa/ and /ua/ respectively. ◌ิว is transcribed as /iu/ and เ◌ียว is transcribed as /iao/.

Consonant Classes

Thai consonants are divided into three classes — high, midle and low. Since it is one of the critical factors in determining a syllable's tone, you must know the consonant class in order to correctly pronounce what you have read.

The names — high, middle and low — of the consonant classes are completely arbitrary. A low consonant may generate a high tone and a high consonant can generate a low tone, etc.

What Determines The Tone

1. Consonant class: whether the initial consonant is high, middle or low.

2. Vowel length: whether short or long.

3. Tone Mark: whether or not there is a tone mark placed above the initial consonant of a syllable. (If the consonant has a superscript vowel, the tone mark is placed above that vowel.)

4. Final consonant: whether sonorant final or stop final.

Seven Vowels That Change Their Forms

The following seven vowels change their forms when they appear in medial position.

Vowels	Final Position	Medial Position
–ะ	กะ /gà/	กัด /gàt/
–ือ	ตือ /dtʉʉ/	ตืน /dtʉʉn/
เ–ะ	เปะ /bpè/	เป็น /bpen/
แ–ะ	แตะ /dè/	แต็ก /dtèk/
โ–ะ	โจะ /jò/	จบ /jòp/
–ัว	อัว /ua/	อวน /uan/
เ–อ	เบอ /bəə/	เบิก /bə̀ək/

Tone Marks

Middle Consonants

Tone Mark	Tone Name	Tone	Examples
่	sĭang èek	*low*	ก่า (gàa)
้	sĭang too	*falling*	ก้า (gâa)
๊	sĭang dtrii	*high*	ก๊า (gáa)
๋	sĭang jàt-dtà-waa	*rising*	ก๋า (gǎa)

High Consonants

Tone Mark	Tone Name	Tone	Examples
่	sĭang èek	*low*	ข่า (kàa)
้	sĭang too	*falling*	ข้า (kâa)

Low Consonants

Tone Mark	Tone Name	Tone	Examples
่	sĭang too	*falling*	ค่า (kâa)
้	sĭang dtrii	*high*	ค้า (káa)

Live and Dead Syllables

A syllable that ends with a short vowel or a stop final consonant is called a <u>dead syllable</u>.

A syllable that ends with a long vowel or a sonorant final consonant is called a <u>live syllable</u>.

Rising tone and its corresponding tone mark ($\overset{+}{-}$) never occur with a dead syllable.

Tone Rules
(In the Absence of Tone Marks)

1. mid consonant with live syllable = mid tone

    e.g.   กา   กาน

2. mid consonant with dead syllable = low tone

    e.g.   กะ   กาบ

3. high consonant with live syllable = rising tone

    e.g.   ขา   ขาน

4. high consonant with dead syllable = low tone

    e.g.   ขะ   ขาบ

5. low consonant with live syllable = mid tone

    e.g.   คา   คาน

6. low consonant with short vowel and dead syllable
    = high tone

    e.g.   คะ   ค้บ

7. low consonant with long vowel and dead syllable
    = falling tone

    e.g.   คาบ

Appendix II
Test and Writing Exercise Answers

Test Answers

Test1

Matching:

1. e	2. j	3. b	4. c	5. g
6. l	7. k	8. h	9. a	10. i

Translation:

1. How are you?
2. (Do you) understand?
3. Is this a newspaper?
4. What's your name?
5. Is this a map or a pencil?

Test 2

Matching:

1. m	2. k	3. n	4. l	5. o
6. e	7. p	8. g	9. b	10. a
11. j	12. q	13. d	14. f	15. h

Translation:

1. The telephone is on the chair.
2. He is Chinese, not Japanese.
3. How much is this?
4. Where is the bathroom?
5. English is very difficult.

Test 3

Matching:

1. j	2. n	3. f	4. a	5. q
6. m	7. b	8 l	9. d	10. p
11. c	12. e	13. h	14 i	15. k

Translation:

1. Where do you work?
2. I like blue cars.
3. Do you like Thai food or Chinese food?
4. Where is he going?
5. You can write Thai very well.

Test 4

Telling Time:

1. 6:15 a.m. or 6:15 p.m.
2. 9:00 p.m.
3. 10:30 a.m. or 4:30 p.m.
4. 2:35 a.m.
5. Exactly 3:00 p.m.
6. 10:50 a.m. or 4:50 p.m.
7. 12:20 p.m. (noon time)
8. 1:05 p.m.
9. 8:20 p.m.
10. 4:00 a.m.
11. 10:00 a.m.
12. Exactly noon.
13. 8:00 p.m.
14. 8:10 a.m.
15. 11:00 a.m.

Translation:

1. I will go to the temple at noon.
2. He has been reading since eleven p.m.
3. We study Thai for three hours.
4. It's now one thirty p.m.
5. I eat breakfast at eight o'clock.

Test 5

Matching:

Days

1. c   2. e   3. f   4. h   5. a   6. d   7. b   8. g

Months

1. i   2. e   3. 1   4. a   5. g   6. h
7. j   8. c   9. f   10. k   11. d   12. b

Test 6

Matching:

1. o   2. a   3. h   4. i   5. 1
6. p   7. n   8. b   9. e   10. k
11. q   12. d   13. c   14. m   15. g

Translation:

1. Now I'm going to the airport.
2. Normally, Mr. Somchai goes to work by train.
3. We want to have a Thai restaurant in America.
4. He has been in Thailand since June.
5. I don't like to listen to music very much.

Test 7

Matching:

1. m   2. h   3. d   4. p   5. j
6. n   7. a   8. o   9. k   10. f
11. c   12. q   13. e   14. b   15. i

Translation:

1. Whose notebook is on the table?
2. I can't swim.

3. I didn't swim.
4. He really misses Thailand.
5. I think that western food is not very delicious.

Test 8

Matching:

1. d   2. m   3. i   4. h   5. e
6. p   7. c   8. a   9. g   10. n
11. k   12. b   13. l   14. j   15. f

Translation:

1. How many times a day do you brush your teeth?
    Twice a day.
2. He has a bad headache. He can't come to work.
3. I wash my hair everyday.
4. Somchai has dimples.
5. You have no brain.

Test 9

Matching:

A.
1. c   2. e   3. d   4. k   5. m
6. l   7. h   8. f   9. b   10. j

B.
1. h   2. j   3. c   4. l   5. g
6. e   7. d   8. f   9. b   10. a

C.
1. k   2. f   3. l   4. b   5. j
6. e   7. i   8. h   9. m   .10. g

Translation:

1. What kind of work does your younger brother do?
2. He is married to a Japanese.
3. Why don't you like Thai food?   Because it's very hot.
4. If I don't have money, I cannot return to Thailand.
5. I think that he already has a family.

Test 10

Matching:
A.

| 1. c | 2. l | 3. i | 4. e | 5. k |
| 6. a | 7. b | 8. f | 9. h | 10. g |

B.

| 1. k | 2. h | 3. e | 4. d | 5. c |
| 6. m | 7. a | 8. j | 9. f | 10. g |

C.

| 1. g | 2. d | 3. m | 4. h | 5. a |
| 6. k | 7. e | 8. b | 9. l | 10. f |

Translation:

1. Which mango is the most delicious?
   I think that this one is the most delicious.
2. How many floors are there at your house?
   There are three.
3. When will the first ship come?
   It will come tomorrow.
4. Yesterday I bought a new watch.
5. There are five elephants at the zoo.

Writing Exercise Answer

Writing Exercise 1

1. ดา   2. โก่   3. ไบ้, ใบ้   4. ตู่
5. เอา   6. โป่   7. เก่า   8. จี้
9. ไฮ้   10. เบ้   11. ไจ,ใจ   12. เต่า
13. โอ   14. ไป   15. กู้   16. โบ่
17. จ่ำ   18. เดา   19. กี่   20. อ้า

Writing Exercise 2

1. บา   2. แกะ   3. เบือ   4. ตุ
5. บอ   6. เจ   7. กิ   8. เจอะ
9. ออ   10. จัวะ   11. เกือ   12. ตอ
13. อือ   14. ปะ   15. กี   16. เตาะ
17. เออ   18. โดะ   19. ดัว   20. เกียะ

Writing Exercise 3

1. จัน   2. เปิด   3. บัง   4. กวม
5. จีด   6. เต็ม   7. ผม   8. ดัง
9. เก็บ   10. ตก   11. ดน   12. เอ็น
13. แด็ม   14. จึง   15. บวม   16. อง
17. เดิน   18. เจ็บ   19. ปวด   20. บวก
21. กั้น   22. จม   23. บั้ง   24. อูด
25. กุ้ง   26. จาม   27. เก่า   28. ตื่น
29. ด้าม   30. อก   31. ตั้น   32. ปีบ

33. ดั้ง   34. บัด   35. บ่าย   36. โอ่ง

37. จ่ำ   38. เจ็บ   38. แกบ   40. จ่าว

Writing Exercise 4

1. ฉา   2. ผะ   3. ฉัน   4. ขอด

5. เสียว   6. ผี   7. แขก   8. เถียง

9. แฝด   10. สอน   11. หุบ   12. ถุง

13. ผม   14. ฝัง   15. หาบ   16. เตะ

17. ฉุน   18. หาย   19. ผัด   20. ขาว

Writing Exercise 5

1. ฉ่อย   2. ผึ้ง   3. ห้วน   4. ขม

5. ผื่น   6. ถ่อย   7. ส่ง   8. ขูด

9. เผย   10. ถาม   11. สวย   12. ฝัง

13. ถี่   14. ฝ่าน   15. ขาย   16. ข้าว

17. ห้อง   18. ฝ้าย   19. ฉาบ   20. เส้น

Writing Exercise 6

1. พา   2. โช   3. รำ,รัม   4. มู

5. เชีย   6. เลีย   7. เชย   8. ทัว

9. เรือ   10. เฟา   11. ที   12. ยอ

13. ฟู   14. เท   15. คอ   16. คือ

17. งา   18. แพ   19. ยำ.ยัม   20. ลา

Writing Exercise 7

1. ม่วง   2. นก   3. ค่ำ, คั้ม   4. ยูง
5. ฟีม   6. นิ้ว   7. มีด   8. ซอง
9. ฟัง   10. แวว   11. ชาม   12. เรียบ
13. พูม   14. ร้าน   15. ฮาบ   16. ว่าง
17. เยื้อง   18. แช่ง   19. คก   20. เพื่อ

Writing Exercise 8

1. หมี่   2. ไหน , ใหน , ไหณ , ใหณ
3. ใหญ่, ไหญ่, ใหย่, ไหย่   4. หนี้ , หณี้
5. หมั่น   6. หลา   7. หวู่
8. โหร่ง   9. หวั่น   10. หรา

About the Author

Benjawan Poomsan Becker (เบญจวรรณ ภูมิแสน เบคเกอร์)
was born in Bangkok and spent her childhood in Yasothon, a small
province in Northeast Thailand. Her family is ethnic Laotian, so
she grew up speaking both Thai and Lao. She graduated from Khon
Kaen University in Thailand in 1990, with a B.A. in English.
Benjawan gained extensive experience teaching Thai to foreigners
while studying for her M.A. in sociology in Japan with the Japan-
Thailand Trade Association and Berlitz Language Schools, and in
the US with Thai temples, Stanford University and private stu-
dents. In 1994 she married Craig Becker. They reside in Berkeley,
California where she continues to write and publish books on the
Thai and Lao languages. She also has a translation and interpreta-
tion business. Her books include "Thai for Beginners", "Thai for
Intermediate Learners", "Thai for Advanced Readers", "Thai für
Angfänger", "Taigo No Kiso" and "Thai-English, English-Thai
Dictionary for Non-Thai Speakers".

If you are interested in wholesale purchases, or distribution of these books outside of Thailand, the USA and Canada, please contact PAIBOON PUBLISHING.
Tel: 1-510-848-7086
Fax: 1-510-848-4521
Email: paiboon@thailao.com
Website: www.thailao.com

สนใจเป็นผู้แทนจำหน่ายหรือขายส่งในประเทศไทย
กรุณาติดต่อสำนักพิมพ์ไพบูลย์ภูมิแสน
ที่หมายเลขโทรศัพท์ 02-509-8632
โทรสาร 02-519-5437

Thai Language Books by Paiboon Publishing

Title: **Thai for Beginners**
Author: Benjawan Poomsan Becker ©1995
Description: Designed for either self-study or classroom use. Teaches all four
                language skills— speaking, listening (when used in conjunction
                with the cassette tapes), reading and writing . Offers clear, easy,
                step-by-step instruction building on what has been previously
                learned. Used by many Thai temples and insitutes in America.
                Cassette tapes available. Paperback. 262 pages. 6" x 8.5"
Book   US$12.95   Stock # 1001
Three Tape Set US$20.00   Stock # 1001T

****

Title: **Thai for Intermediate Learners**
Author: Benjawan Poomsan Becker ©1998
Description: The continuation of *Thai for Beginners* . Users are expected to be
                able to read basic Thai language. There is transliteration when
                new words are introduced. Teaches reading, writing and speaking
                at a higher level. Keeps students interested with cultural facts about
                Thailand. Helps expand your Thai vocabulary in a systematic way.
                Two casettes available. Paperback. 220 pages. 6" x 8.5"
Book   US$12.95   Stock # 1002
Two Tape Set   US$15.00   Stock # 1002T

****

Title: **Thai for Advanced Readers**
Author: Benjawan Poomsan Becker ©2000
Description: A book that helps students practice reading Thai at an advanced level.
                It contains reading exercises, short essays, newspaper articles, cutural
                and historical facts about Thailand and miscellaneous information about
                the Thai language. Students need to be able to read basic Thai. Two
                casette tapes available. Paperback. 210 pages. 6" x 8.5"
Book   US$12.95   Stock # 1003
Two Tape Set   US$15.00   Stock # 1003T

****

Title: **Thai for Lovers**
Author: Nit & Jack Ajee ©1999
Description: An ideal book for lovers. A short cut to romantic communication
                in Thailand. There are useful sentences with their Thai translations
                throughout the book. You won't find any Thai language book more
                fun and user-friendly. **Rated R!**
                Two casettes available. Paperback. 190 pages. 6" x 8.5"
Book   US$13.95   Stock #: 1004
Two Tape Set   US$17.00   Stock #: 1004T

Title:	**Thai for Gay Tourists**
Author:	Saksit Pakdeesiam ©2001
Description:	The ultimate language guide for gay and bisexual men visiting Thailand. Lots of gay oriented language, culture, commentaries and other information. Instant sentences for convenient use by gay visitors. Fun and sexy. The best way to communicate with your Thai gay friends and partners! **Rated R!**
	Cassette tapes available. Paperback. 220 pages. 6" x 8.5"
Book	US$13.95 Stock # 1007
Two Tape Set	US$17.00 Stock # 1007T

****

Deutschsprachiges Lehrbuch über die Thai-Sprache von Paiboon Publishing

Titel:	**Thai für Anfänger**
Autor:	Benjawan Poomsan Becker ©2000
Beschreibung:	Für das selbständige Lernen zu Hause oder für den Gebrauch im Klassenzimmer. Vermittelt Grundkenntnisse der Thai-Sprache. Das Buch kann mit den entsprechenden Tonbandkassetten kombiniert werden. Bietet klare und einfache Instruktionen, die Schritt für Schritt auf bereits Erlerntem aufbauen. Wird von zahlreichen Thai-Tempeln und Sprachinstituten in Amerika benutzt.
	Tonbandkassetten erhältlich. Taschenbuch. 245 Seiten. 15 cm x 22 cm
Buch	US$13.95 Lagernummer 1005
Kassetten (3er Set)	US$20.00 Lagernummer 1005T

****

All books are fun and easy to use.
Mit unseren Büchern macht das Lernen Spass.

Thai-English, English-Thai Dictionary
for Non-Thai Speakers

Author: Benjawan Poomsan Becker
             ©2002
Paperback: 658 pages
Size: 6" x 8.5"
Price: US$15.00
Stock #   1008

This practical dictionary is designed to help English speakers communicate in Thai. It is equally useful for those who can read the Thai alphabet and those who can't. Most Thai-English dictionaries either use Thai script exclusively for the Thai entries (making them difficult for westerners to use) or use only phonetic transliteration (making it impossible to look up a word in Thai script). This dictionary solves these problems by dividing the entries into three sections: Section One [English-Phonetic-Thai], Section Two [Phonetic-Thai-English] and Section Three [Thai-Phonetic-English]. The transliteration system is the same as that used in Paiboon Publishing's other books. You will find most of the vocabulary you are likely to need in everyday life, including basic medical, cultural, political and scientific terms.

Here are some of the features:

❐ Consistent and accurate phonetic transcription of Thai sounds for those unable to read the Thai alphabet
❐ A comprehensive guide to pronunciation
❐ Thai script for those who read Thai
❐ All entries organized in three easy to use sections
❐ Thai alphabet guide showing different styles of Thai script to help you read shop signs and newspaper headlines

It's the ONE Dictionary You Can Really Use!

PAIBOON PUBLISHING
ORDER FORM

QTY.	ITEM NO.	NAME OF ITEM	ITEM PRICE	TOTAL

Delivery Charges for First Class and Airmail

	USA and Canada	Other Countries
Up to $25.00	US$3.95	US$8.95
$25.01-$50.00	US$4.95	US$11.95
$50.01-$75.00	US$6.25	US$15.25
$75.01-$100.00	US$7.75	US$18.75
Over $100.00	FREE	US$18.75

Merchandise Total _____

CA residents add 8.25% sales tax _____

Delivery Charge (See Chart at Left) _____

Total _____

Method of Payment ❏ Check   ❏ Money Order   Make payable to Paiboon Publishing

Charge to: ❏ Visa   ❏ Master Card   ❏ Amex

Card # _____   Exp. Date _____/____

Signature_____   Tel _____

Name _____   Date _____

Address _____

_____

_____

Email Address _____

Mail order is for orders outside of Thailand only.
Send your order and payment to: Paiboon Publishing
PMB 192, 1442A Walnut Street, Berkeley, CA 94709 USA
Tel: 1-510-848-7086 Fax: 1-510-848-4521
Email: paiboon@thailao.com Website: www.thailao.com
Allow 2-3 weeks for delivery.

PAIBOON

PUBLISHING